Project Management Institute

Governance and Communities of PMOs

Monique Aubry, PhD, MPM
School of Business and Management,
University of Quebec at Montreal, Canada

Ralf Müller, DBA, MBA, PMP
Umeå School of Business, Umeå University, Sweden
BI Norwegian Business School, Norway

Johannes Glückler, PhD
University of Heidelberg, Germany

Library of Congress Cataloging-in-Publication Data

Aubry, Monique.
    Governance and communities of PMOs / Monique Aubry, Ralf Müller, Johannes Glückler.
        p. cm.
    Includes bibliographical references.
    ISBN 978-1-935589-48-8 (alk. paper)
    1. Project management. 2. Communication in organizations. 3. Organizational learning.
4. Knowledge management. 5. Community organization. I. Müller, Ralf, 1957- II. Glückler,
Johannes. III. Title.
    HD69.P75.A928 2012
    658.4'04—dc23

2011050791

Published by: Project Management Institute, Inc.
                     14 Campus Boulevard
                     Newtown Square, Pennsylvania 19073-3299 USA
                     Phone: +610-356-4600
                     Fax: +610-356-4647
                     Email: customercare@pmi.org
                     Internet: www.PMI.org

PMI Publications welcomes corrections and comments on its books. Please feel free to send comments on typographical, formatting, or other errors. Simply make a copy of the relevant page of the book, mark the error, and send it to: Book Editor, PMI Publications, 14 Campus Boulevard, Newtown Square, PA 19073-3299 USA.

To inquire about discounts for resale or educational purposes, please contact the PMI Book Service Center.

                     PMI Book Service Center
                     P.O. Box 932683, Atlanta, GA 31193-2683 USA
                     Phone: 1-866-276-4764 (within the U.S. or Canada) or +1-770-280-4129
                     (globally)
                     Fax: +1-770-280-4113
                     Email: info@bookorders.pmi.org

Table of Contents

List of Figures

List of Tables

Executive Summary

The coexistence of multiple project management offices (PMOs) in large organizations is actually a common situation. However, this is the first academic research (to our knowledge) on this phenomenon, even if it brings major challenges to managers involved in the organizational project management. The idea of communities of PMOs emerged from the ground as an avenue for organizations to get more outcomes with less investment in the management of many portfolios of projects. This research is aimed at getting a better understanding of this phenomenon.

This research is part of a research program on PMOs undertaken at the University of Quebec at Montreal, so it builds on what was already known on single PMOs. This specific international research team included two researchers from the project management community, who are already involved in PMOs' research. The team also included a professor outside the field who comes from social geography and innovation. Altogether, the team has a diversity of competences that enlighten the phenomenon with new lenses.

This research deliberately took a knowledge management perspective. These are the assumptions:

- Innovation is essential for organizations to grow and survive.
- Organizational learning is essential to innovate.
- Community of practices is a good approach to organizational learning.

The initial conceptual framework was built on three complementary theories: network theory, transaction cost theory, and community of practice theory. The framework reflected the pluralism of perspectives that are needed now to take into account complex organizational phenomena, with communities of PMOs being one of them. This framework has been revised after analysis of the research results.

A mixed method approach was used in this research, combining four in-depth case studies and a social network analysis. This combination provided two complementary views and helped with understanding the phenomenon. Four organizations participated in this research, one each from the telecommunications, health care, financial, and pharmaceutical industries and from three continents (Asia, Europe, and North America).

These are the key findings from the case studies:

- Generally speaking, multiple PMOs appeared to be rather complex phenomena within their organizations.
- There seems to be an alignment between context, governance, and structure of relationships.

- Surprisingly, PMOs at a top level focus on compliance to standards, while PMOs at the lower level focus on outcome. This result contradicts the general assumption that PMOs at the top level are business and strategy oriented, while PMOs at the lower level are methodology and tactically oriented.
- Networks of PMOs were rather strong in their controlling role.
- Mechanistic PMOs networks are found in case companies in hyper-competitive markets, whereas organic PMO networks are found in stable markets.
- True communities of PMOs are rather rare.

These are the key findings from the within-case analyses:

- Control and serving roles are the most frequent PMO roles.
- PMOs in partnering roles are more likely to share knowledge within a community of PMOs.

These are the key findings from social network analysis:

- People tend to overestimate their importance as knowledge providers.
- Although project managers widely appreciated the role of the PMO, the network analysis found that the PMO did not occupy a pronounced role in dyadic knowledge transfer within the project management community.
- Ninety percent of all interpersonal knowledge transfer relations are within clusters of project managers. Only the most innovative employees exchanged knowledge across these clusters.
- Time constraints were reported as the primary barrier to more effective knowledge transfer.
- Some managers suggested to increase the involvement of people from other functional departments in projects and case studies (e.g., to analyze the advantages and disadvantages from one case). This suggestion reflects the high fragmentation of knowledge between the PMO managers and their virtual communities of project managers, which was identified in the network analysis.

A few major items stem from these key findings, and they will be discussed further:

1. Communities of PMOs are not frequently found in organizations, for two major reasons: (1) the top-down control that maintains a Taylorism paradigm and focuses mainly on explicit knowledge; and (2) a lack of the sense of a community. This opens up opportunities to better manage knowledge through networks of PMOs for them to become true communities of PMOs. This reinforces the role of managers (e.g., PMO manager, portfolio or program manager) and allows for learning related slack times and the creation of an environment where knowledge creation and sharing will happen.
2. A new component has been added to the conceptual framework mentioned previously to reflect the impact of relationships between PMOs on organizational performance in terms of slack and innovativeness as well as ambidexterity. This calls for managerial competences to articulate exploitation of what we already know and calls for exploration for new learning for better innovation.

3. A particular pattern was observed in the four PMO networks investigated. We labeled it the bagel metaphor. Here, the central PMO works within a strong controlling role with other PMOs, either within functional or business units. However, the other PMOs ignore this central PMO when serving or partnering among PMOs. The central PMO is in an "ivory tower," while others evolve in their own network. This creates a hole at the center of the network. In a knowledge economy, this pattern might not be the best one to develop and provide contributions to organizational performance. More than this, being disconnected from reality, this central PMO might not have access to the reality of projects, which gets it "out of sync" with organizational reality and makes it communicate inappropriately with those working in projects. In conclusion, our findings show that networks of PMOs exist but communities of PMOs are still rare. This represents an opportunity for future development within organizations to get more from the knowledge creation and sharing in project management.

Acknowledgments

The authors wish to thank Project Management Institute (PMI), the Per and Eivor Wikström Foundation, as well as the Research Council at Umeå University for their financial support.

The authors also wish to express their gratitude to the four organizations and their employees who participated in this research. They provided rich case studies from which new knowledge on PMOs could be developed and shared with the project management community.

Last, but certainly not least, the authors would like to express their gratitude to Jingting Shao, Heike Dennhard, Tamara Tsaturyan, and Robert Panitz for their contributions to the data collection and analysis stages of this research. Their work was crucial for the success of the studies.

Chapter 1

Introduction[1]

1.1 Context of This Research

The real impetus for undertaking this research came from the participation of one author in a workshop on project management offices (PMOs) in a large European governmental ministry. The reason to hold this event was to group as much as possible the dozens of PMO directors under the theme of Community of PMOs. The leadership of this initiative came from a top executive with a clear mandate of making some "order in the house" in the management of a very large project portfolio. In this ministry, as in many large organizations, there are multiple PMOs, each one with its specific mandate and often in different functional units and without mechanisms that would break the silos between them. Making people talk together is expected to generate economies by preventing them from *constantly reinventing the wheel*. The phenomenon of multiple PMOs is clearly present in these organizations and this research aims at providing some understanding of it.

The PMO as an organizational phenomenon keeps the interest within the project management research field. An indicator of this situation is the noticeable recent research on this subject presented at research conferences (Aubry, 2009; L. Crawford, 2010; Dietrich, Artto, & Kujala, 2010; Pinto, Cota, & Levin, 2010; Unger, Gemünden, & Aubry, 2011; Winch, Meunier, & Head, 2010), as well as in specialized project management journals (Artto, Kulvik, Poskela & Turkulainen, 2011; Aubry, Müller, Hobbs, & Blomquist, 2010; Hurt & Thomas, 2009; Pellegrinelli & Garagna, 2009). This statement can also be extended to other project management subjects that pertain to the organizational level (as opposed to the project level) such as program, portfolio, business projects, etc.

One interpretation of the vigor of this research trend suggests that research has not yet delivered those answers needed to help professionals solving organizational project management problems. In a more critical approach, it can also be interpreted as a fashion nurtured, among others, by researchers themselves. To avoid the fashion effect and the fade out, L. Crawford (2010) suggested going back to what PMOs really do and focus on their

---

[1]The content of this monograph presents an improved version of papers presented at the 2010 PMI® Research and Education Conference (Aubry, Müller, & Glückler, 2010) and at the 2011 IRNOP Research Conference (Müller, Aubry, & Glückler, 2011). Correspondence concerning this article should be addressed to Monique Aubry, School of Business and Management, University of Quebec at Montreal, Montreal (Quebec), H3C 3P8, Canada. Email: aubry.monique@uqam.ca

functions. In parallel, project management structures continue to evolve. When considering a PMO as an organizational innovation, Hobbs, Aubry, and Thuillier (2008) showed that the PMO is still in a ferment era. The phenomenon is not stabilized yet.

Until recently, empirical research has primarily looked at individual PMOs, often because organizations had only implemented a single PMO to serve project management needs. Some of the well-researched questions related to PMO models (Hobbs & Aubry, 2010), performance (Dai & Wells, 2004), or frequent transformations (Aubry, Hobbs, Müller, & Blomquist, 2011; Hurt & Thomas, 2009). With some exceptions, however, there is only limited quantitative validation to concepts and propositions regarding PMO performance (Dai & Wells, 2004), PMO typologies (Hobbs & Aubry, 2008, 2011), or patterns of change (Aubry et al., 2010).

More recently, large organizations have started to implement multiple concurrent PMOs, each one having a different mandate, functions, and characteristics. PMOs have been implemented at different levels within the organizational hierarchy (J. K. Crawford, 2010) and in business units and functional units, but typically, it seems that they emerge without any global strategic orientation. Organizations (such as the ministry example provided at the very beginning of the Introduction) are now searching for a better articulation between these PMOs and within their overall governance structure. Clearly, with proliferation of projects (and with it proliferation of structures, processes, and tools), they are looking for efficiency in project management. However, research has not been conducted on the phenomenon of coexistence of multiple PMOs.

One promising avenue to explore the multiple PMOs phenomenon is to turn towards knowledge management. Knowledge management is recognized as an important issue for organizations to succeed in a highly competitive environment. Today's knowledge-based economy calls for mechanisms to share knowledge. This is particularly true in the context of internationalization of business where services or products are developed, managed, or supported in multiple countries. This is also true for national companies that compete in a global market. The issue of making more with less is at stake to reuse good practices, support innovative practice, and prevent the reinvention of the wheel (Glückler, 2008, 2011). For project-based organizations, this represents a major challenge, because projects are temporary organizations (Lundin & Söderholm, 1995; Turner & Müller, 2003), and knowledge evaporates after disbanding of the project team at project end. Moreover, projects and project management have come to play a central role in international economic growth (Bredillet, Yatim, & Ruiz, 2010). Therefore, project-based organizations should be highly concerned about knowledge management. One promising approach is to explore the role of PMOs and communities of PMOs as a locus of learning.

From the project management literature, knowledge management can be viewed from the perspective of two different levels of analysis: project or organizational level. Research undertaken at the project level has mainly explored the transfer of knowledge from one project to another. Perspectives taken by researchers include, among others: post-project reviews (Williams, 2007), social practices (Bresnen, Edelman, Newell, Scarbrough, & Swan, 2003; Sense & Badham, 2008), and quality management (Kotnour, 2000). At the organizational level, Bredillet (2004) proposed an overview on knowledge management, organizational learning, and learning organization. Other researchers have drawn attention to particular perspectives such as human resource management (Bellini & Canonico, 2008; Keegan & Turner, 2001) or nonfinancial capital (Arthur, DeFillippi, & Jones, 2001). In addition, some authors have looked at knowledge sharing between industries (Fernie, Green, Weller, & Newcombe, 2003), while others have examined the methods to capture and validate relevant knowledge (Abril & Müller, 2009).

In light of the wide variety of PMO roles and activities listed previously, organizations start to distribute the many roles over several PMO entities, which leads to the coexistence of multiple PMOs, particularly in large organizations. As exemplified previously, PMOs are not autonomous or isolated units within an organization but they are frequently intertwined with other PMOs in the same corporation. This is in line with results from recent research showing an increase in the interdependencies between PMOs after a PMO structural change (Aubry et al., 2011).

In line with this development, the governance of these multi-PMO settings has become an emerging topic. PMOs are part of the structures for project and project management governance in organizations. This is independent of their specific role, mandate, or location. PMOs and other project governance entities, such as Steering Committees, program and portfolio management, form what has been defined in organizational project management as "a new sphere of management where dynamic structures in the firm are articulated as means to implement corporate objectives through projects in order to maximize value" (Aubry, Hobbs, & Thuillier, 2007, p. 332).

What we now observe in large organizations is the creation of communities of PMOs aimed at learning and sharing knowledge in the management of projects. These communities form one pattern of organizational project management. The community of PMOs consists of internal networks of PMOs that cross the organizational boundaries. Networks can be formed implicitly or explicitly to create value by sharing knowledge in the management of projects.

In this monograph, the authors borrow from the theory of community of practice (CoP) (Lave & Wenger, 1991) to explore the PMOs' social networks as communities of practice. This approach offers the opportunity to build not only on the grouping role of PMOs around multiple projects but also on the practice of project management and its practitioners. This phenomenon of community of practice has previously been acknowledged within the field of project management research. A rapid look at the publications from the three specialized academic journals for project management shows that since 2002, 40 articles have been published. Interestingly, the Project Management Association of Japan introduced the management of a community of practice as part of the project and program management (Project Management Association of Japan, 2008). However, none of these papers addresses the role of the PMOs in the making and sharing of knowledge on project management practices.

Following what has been said previously on the current organizational context, the main objective of the present research is to provide an understanding of the role PMOs could take on in knowledge management, in terms of islands, networks, or community of PMOs.

These objectives are addressed by answering the following questions:

- How can communities of PMOs be described?
- How do PMOs interact?
- How does knowledge flow between PMOs and project managers?
- What are the related project governance mechanisms?

The Unit of Analysis is the relationship between PMOs in an organization.

The present research project is part of a larger research program, which will be presented next.

1.2 This Research Within the PMO Research Program at UQAM

This monograph aims at exploring the multiple PMOs phenomenon. The research is part of a research program on PMOs at the Project Management Research Chair at the University of Quebec at Montreal (UQAM; www.pmchair.uqam.ca). As shown in Table 1-1, the research program includes six phases, with the present study as the latest phase. The first four phases focused on single PMOs, and the fifth one focused on the PMOs' transformation. This last phase is the only study having multiple PMOs as objects of analysis.

The underlying value in the management of this research project is to stay in contact with the practitioner's community in project management, following the approach of "engaged scholarship" (Van de Ven, 2007). Case studies help maintain the proximity between practitioners and researchers, and workshops, held at UQAM's Project Management Research Chair, have presented and discussed preliminary results. Responses at these events confirmed practitioners' interest in exploring this subject and showed the complexity and dynamics of relationships between PMOs, as well their expected contribution to knowledge management within organizations.

This book is structured as follows. Chapter 2 presents the literature review and provides a conceptual framework that will be used to explore the phenomenon of multiple PMOs within large organizations. Research design and methodology are presented in Chapter 3. The research adopted a combination of case studies and social network analysis (SNA) to provide rich design adapted to this explorative research. The four case studies descriptions are found in Chapter 4. Findings appear in Chapters 5 and 6. From the analysis of the relationships between PMOs, Chapter 5 suggests a role model of PMOs linked with innovativeness. Chapter 6 presents the findings from the SNA that challenge the PMO role. Chapter 7 discusses the findings. Finally, Chapter 8 presents the conclusion, including research limitations and paths for future research.

Table 1-1. Research Program on PMOs at UQAM

Phase of the Research Program	Period	Description
1	2005–2006	Two descriptive surveys of 500 PMOs aimed at providing a realistic portrait of the population of PMOs.
2	2006	The development of a rich conceptual model to guide further investigation.
3	2006–2007	In-depth case studies of 12 PMOs in 4 organizations aimed at understanding the dynamics surrounding PMOs in their organizational context.
4	2008	Analysis of the data from phases I, II, & III and production of a monograph published by PMI.
5	2008–2010	Identifying the forces driving the frequent changes in PMOs.
6	**2009–2011**	**Governance and communities of PMOs.**

Chapter 2

Literature Review
and Conceptual Framework

This research deals with multiple PMOs and more specifically with their capacity for active participation in knowledge creation and diffusion in project management. This is only possible when PMOs are involved in relationships with others. In this chapter, relevant literature is reviewed under three themes: circulation of knowledge from a single PMO perspective, structural arrangement between multiple PMOs, and the governance challenge. From this review of literature, the last section presents a conceptual framework to understand communities of PMOs.

Past research on PMOs mainly looked at PMOs as one instance at a time. Two major conclusions can be drawn. First, research has shown an extreme variety of PMO structures, mandates, and functions (Hobbs & Aubry, 2010). This variation, however, is not easily explained using usual contingency variables such as industry or region (Hobbs & Aubry, 2008). Recent cluster analysis on 500 PMO descriptions provide empirically grounded PMOs typology based on multiple variables (Hobbs & Aubry, 2011). Second, PMOs are changing frequently. Recent research confirmed temporality as a key characteristic of PMOs and that this temporality could be better understood within the external and internal dynamics of the organization (Aubry et al., 2011). Results confirm that external and internal factors and idiosyncrasies drive the transformation of one PMO to the next. The temporality dimension reflects an organizational ambidexterity (Gibson & Birkinshaw, 2004) between transformation and sustainability. Both coexist in the sense that sustainability should be understood within the transformation process (Hurt & Thomas, 2009). Extreme variation and frequent changes raise particular challenges when looking at knowledge sharing, because patterns of knowledge sharing are difficult to identify within the wider variety and at the particular moment they occur within this variety (thus, in space and time).

2.1 How Do Project Management Offices Support the Circulation of Knowledge?

A descriptive PMO model has recently been proposed to make sense of the variety of configurations that are found in reality (Hobbs & Aubry, 2010). This model includes three main groups of elements to describe the PMO: organizational context, structural characteristics, and functions within the PMO mandate. Within this model, organizational knowledge management refers to one specific function. It includes such activities as these:

- Monitor and control the performance of the PMO;
- Manage archives of project documentation;
- Conduct post-project reviews or post-mortems;
- Conduct project audits;
- Implement and manage database of lessons learned; and
- Implement and manage risk database.

The organizational knowledge management function is one of the least important when compared with others (Hobbs & Aubry, 2010). This low result should be looked at in the light of other research undertaken on knowledge management at the project level. Williams (2008), for example, showed that project team documentation on lessons learned was poorly done. Often members of a team are dispatched to a new project, not waiting for the current one to close. It is well acknowledged that lessons learned are a good means to transfer knowledge, but it is just not done. This is at the individual project level, but there is an assumption that transfer of knowledge is not managed better at the PMO level.

However, there is another perspective when looking at knowledge management in the context of the PMO. Seminal work from Nonaka and Takeuchi (1995) proposed a framework based on the distinction between explicit knowledge (e.g., documents, patents, statutes) and implicit knowledge (the individual know-how as a capability or competence to solve problems). Tacit knowledge is difficult to articulate or to explain and, therefore, hard to transfer in the pure sense of duplication (Gertler, 2003; Nonaka & von Krogh, 2009). Within projects, explicit knowledge can often be related to the project life cycle (Project Management Institute, 2008). However, tacit knowledge is created as learning (Kotnour, 1999), focusing on the active actor being responsible for its own progression instead of focusing on the object of knowledge (Brown & Duguid, 2001). In other words, "people do not simply learn about, they also learn to be" (Bruner, 1996, as cited in Brown & Duguid, 2001, p. 200). Learning in action (rather than after the fact) makes the practice at the heart of knowledge.

Indeed, the PMO function of organizational learning should be understood not only through explicit and codified knowledge (e.g., databases), but also as including implicit knowledge that develops while performing functions under the PMO's mandate (e.g., community of practices). This is essential to capture the dynamics of the action of learning. This can be observed within a single PMO but it becomes more salient when considering multiple PMOs. The emerging phenomenon of multiple PMOs working together raises questions about knowledge, learning, and practice in the social networks of project managers.

2.2 Multiple PMOs: Islands, Networks, or Communities?

The co-existence of multiple PMOs within an organization is generally an indicator of a strategy of intense development and innovation. Moreover, while projects cross the lines of individual functional or business units, each individual PMO may form new cross-organizational ties through their multidisciplinary projects. This section addresses how PMOs relate to each other by forming an isolated island, a network, or a community.

2.2.1 Usefulness of the Metaphor of Island

This metaphor of an island is used here in reference to the isolated position of the island from any continent and surrounded by water (Island, n.d.). Similarly, an organizational entity could be isolated from the rest of the organization when it is almost impossible to interact with people outside this unit. This unit can be perceived as being turned toward itself and impermeable to communications with others. Instead of water, this unit is surrounded by its own cultural boundary, value, and power, which constitute a barrier to others. Engwall (2003) referred to this metaphor to justify the need of considering the context in the management of projects. This island metaphor could describe functional units in mechanist bureaucracy configuration as defined by Mintzberg (1989). Following Mintzberg, each function in this configuration has a narrow specialization and is encouraged to build its own empire leading to communication and coordination problems. Each unit forms a unique island, or isolated organizational branch, difficult to link together.

This is exactly what Burns and Stalker (1994) observed and they argue for an organic structure for innovative activities rather than a hierarchal functional structure adapted to well known and repetitive tasks. Innovation and more generally projects call for intense interactions between the project's actors and flexible structures such as networks (Powell, 1990), N-Form (Hedlund, 1994), molecular (Morabito, Sack, & Bhate, 1999), cellular (Miles, Snow, Mathews, Miles, & Coleman, 1997), or project-based (Pettigrew & Massini, 2003). Since the intensification of numbers of projects since the 1980s, organizations have adopted these innovative forms of organizing while keeping at the same time the organizational hierarchy (Pettigrew & Massini, 2003).

In the project management literature, project-based structures are often described under four basic approaches: functional, matrix, projectized, and network (Larson, 2004). Problems related to functional structures are, among others, poor integration and slow progression, both associated with lack of communication among functional groups. The three other approaches cross over the functional boundaries. Yet, all these alternative structures break the orthodoxy of a unique organizational structure (Turner & Keegan, 1999) and, in doing so, break the individual silos or islands.

However, isolation should not be always considered as a *wrong* type of organization. For example, in innovation strategy, it happens that a unit is deliberately isolated from the rest of the organization to avoid the inertia of the formal organization and to provide organizational autonomy that is associated with flexibility (Day & Schoemaker, 2000). However, even in this situation, these authors suggested that communications between the formal organization and the autonomous unit should be maintained by keeping the strengths and limiting the weaknesses.

Yet, an isolated entity not entering into relations with others would not serve, at least explicitly, the purpose of knowledge creation and diffusion. Moreover, contributions from multiple (and sometimes divergent) sources of knowledge enrich understanding, as suggested by stakeholder theory within the field of organization theory (Freeman, Harrison, Wicks, Parmar, & De Colle, 2010) and more specifically in the field of project management (Doloi, 2011). Organizing for knowledge should encourage dialogue through a diversity of views including strategy, structure, and processes (Brown & Duguid, 1998; Denis, Langley, &

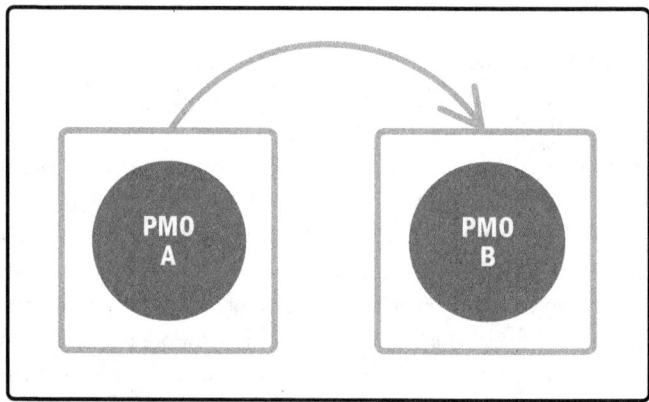

Figure 2-1. PMOs as Isolated Islands

Rouleau, 2007; Hedlund, 1994; Miles et al., 1997). This is also true when theorizing in the field of project management (Söderlund, 2010). The contributions of PMOs to organizational performance benefit from being assessed through the diversity of values (Aubry & Hobbs, 2011; Aubry, Richer, Lavoie-Tremblay, & Cyr, in press).

On the other side of the coin, islands of knowledge are already acknowledged as a characteristic of innovative firms. Hagström, Sölvell, and Hedlund (1999) suggested a three-dimensional model of internal structure of a firm: position, action, and knowledge. The knowledge structure is based upon the concept of islands of knowledge. These islands combine and recombine from everywhere in the structure forming archipelagos. It includes cognitive precepts and skills. This knowledge structure is relatively horizontal, flat, temporary, and circular. In the same vein, Glückler (2011) referred to islands of expertise when he explored the case of a technology service firm. Islands connected together contribute to the transfer of knowledge between internationally distributed centers. Being an island is not a problem per se. What really matters are the connections between these islands.

Turning now to PMOs, Figure 2-1 illustrates PMOs as isolated islands. They exist within thick boundaries that isolate them from each other and from the rest of the organization. In this example, the PMO A developed new knowledge with its internal resources and, then, delivered the result to the PMO B. Despite the high level of expertise of these resources, it is more likely that the PMO A managed without the potential pool of knowledge from diverse stakeholders.

Organizational units that behave as isolated islands are not likely to be expected to have strong relationships with the rest of the organization. So do PMOs. Consequently, they may not contribute much to knowledge management and innovation. However, islands might be a good structural choice depending on strategy and context, but connecting these islands will enhance knowledge management

2.2.2 Networks

While the metaphor of PMOs as islands illustrates the notion of separate and often isolated units in an organization, the concept of the network stresses a sense of connectivity and exchange between the units. In contrast to an archipelago (Hagström et al., 1999) of dispersed and at best loosely related islands, we contend that PMOs may engage in manifold relationships with each other to divide management labor, to transfer resources, and to realize synergies from joint learning and innovation. Situations of interrelated actors are typically analyzed through a network perspective. This section builds on network theory and suggests that different types of relationships contribute differently to knowledge management within a network. This leads to the definition of three roles for PMOs in a network and the identification of their impact on knowledge management. A comprehensive review of the literature on network theory is outside the scope of this monograph. The authors' intention is to provide only the key elements to explain the phenomenon of communities of PMOs. In the context of organizations' studies, networks are theorized in at least two different ways: networks as a governance form and networks as structures of transactional relationships.

Networks as a governance form. The governance approach theorizes networks as a specific form of coordination between economic agents that differs from markets and hierarchies (Powell, 1990; Williamson, 1991). Here, a network is usually defined "as any collection of actors ($N > 2$) that pursue repeated, enduring exchange relations with one another and, at the same time, lack a legitimate organizational authority to arbitrate and resolve disputes that may arise during the exchange" (Podolny & Page, 1998, p. 59). Networks differ from markets and hierarchies in that transactions and relationships are coordinated through trust, reciprocity, and partnership. While market exchanges are usually based on arms-length, price-driven transactions, which are often anonymous. Hierarchies organize transactions around authority and control, and networks provide a third governance style. Despite its important contribution to understanding networks as a distinct quality of governance, this approach has some limitations. It tends to overemphasize trust and reciprocity and to disregard rivalry and competition. Networks are not an end in itself but rather a means for corporations to seek profit (Sayer, 2001). Moreover, the governance approach limits the notion of networks to enduring forms of inter-firm cooperation and thus implicitly impedes an understanding of markets as networks (White, 2002) or firms as networks (e.g., Glückler, 2011).

Networks as structures of relationships. Rather than considering networks as a specific quality of governance, the second approach analyzes networks as patterns of relationships that may be studied and theorized both within and between organizations and markets. In its elementary version, a social network is a specific set of relations among a defined set of actors—individuals or organizations—with the additional property that the characteristics of these relations as a whole may be used to interpret the social behavior of the actors involved (Mitchell, 1969, p. 2). Within this perspective, networks are interpreted as both consequences of individual agency and as constituents of social categories such as identity as well as social opportunities for strategic and collective action (e.g., White, 2008; Burt, 1992; Nohria, 1992). With regard to organization studies, network theories seek to understand the enabling and constraining effects of network structure on individual and collective action. Moreover, network theory aims at explaining the social and economic opportunities and benefits of network structure (Granovetter, 2005). This approach to network theory often uses methods of social network analysis to describe the structural characteristics of networks in terms of their connectivity, density, centralization, fragmentation, center-periphery patterns, etc. (Kilduff & Tsai, 2003). Apart from theorizing the morphology of the network, the social situations and opportunities that actors enjoy within a network are also analyzed at the level of individual positions (e.g., gatekeepers, brokers, clique members, fringe actors) and structural roles.

The quality of relationship in hierarchical networks. The analysis of multiple PMOs in an organization, which is the focus of this monograph, follows the second approach to networks as structures of relationships. This research project is the first to explicitly explore the interrelations and connectivity between multiple PMOs in an organization. Do multiple PMOs represent islands in an organizational archipelago of project management? Or do PMOs form a network of transactional relationships through which resources and experiences are exchanged? To pursue this empirical question, it is necessary to develop a methodology in which the actors as well the kinds of relationships between these actors are defined.

Project management offices build the nodes of the network. PMOs are the organizational units responsible for a set of functions and tasks that they fulfill for project managers on the one hand and upper management on the other. Apart from these relations, this research conjectures that PMOs also maintain transactional relations among each other. In a hierarchical network, three fundamental relationships can be distinguished: an organizational unit can act as a pure service unit, others are management units that directly control and evaluate the performance, and others may exchange in mutual partnership. The central difference between these three ideal roles is the hierarchical vs. partnership dimension in their relations: management authority is a dominating role (controlling), service support responds to demand and is a complementary or even dependent role (serving), and cooperation reflects a collegial role of partnership (partnership). These three relationships are illustrated in the following using two units A and B for simplification (see Figure 2-2). In reality, relationships happen between many units.

In a *controlling* relationship, unit A executes management authority over unit B. This type of relationship is comparable to the traditional hierarchical management approach

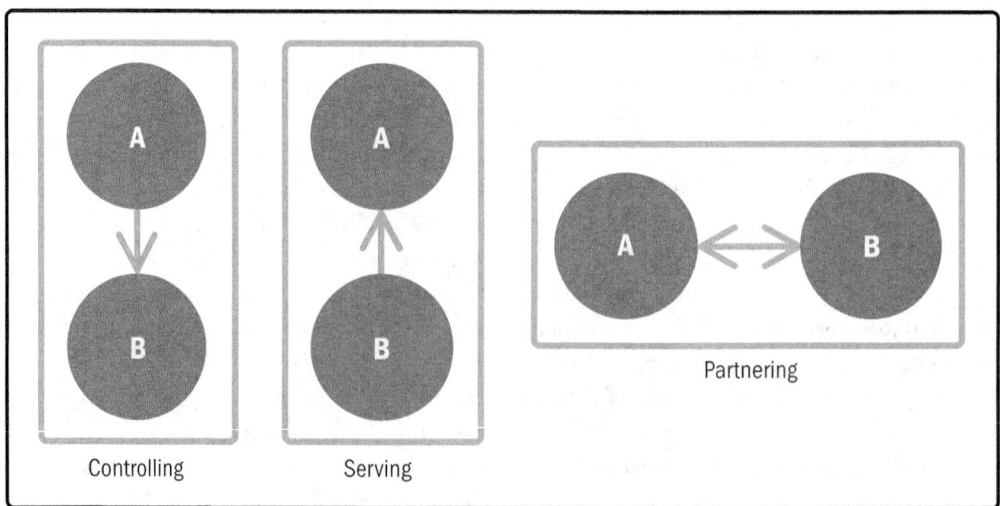

Figure 2-2. Three Types of Relationships in Hierarchical Networks

where the superior level is sending information to the lower level and then is receiving results back that can be judged as satisfactory or not (Galbraith, 1977). In the *serving* relationship, unit B works for, or provides a service to unit A, as shown by the arrow pointing upward. Finally, the third example in Figure 2-2 illustrates the *partnering* relationship, in which units A and B transact in a situation of collegial equality. In this situation, it is more likely that there is no asymmetry in information and that trust more easily develops between them. These fundamental types of relationships promise to be useful categories to develop a relational typology of PMOs.

A typology of PMO roles in the network. Based upon the types of relationship identified, three roles of PMOs are suggested in this section. PMOs entail a number of characteristics that make it a challenging phenomenon to understand. PMOs are extremely heterogeneous—they vary in size, mandate, functions, etc.—and very ephemeral in nature. One of the few larger survey-based studies on PMOs found that the majority of observed PMOs were implemented within the last 24 months only (Hobbs & Aubry, 2010). Given the volatility and context-dependency of PMOs, a number of studies tried to detect underlying commonalities and generalize concrete ideal types of PMOs (Hobbs & Aubry, 2008, 2011). However, most of these typologies focused on characteristics or attributes of PMOs. The present study takes a different approach. First, it focuses on the relationships that a PMO establishes with its intra-organizational environment rather than its internal characteristics. Second, the typology aims at identifying real types rather than ideal types to support management practice.

This research takes a role perspective to understand PMOs as part of knowledge management. A role describes a set of mutual expectations between two actors about their patterns of behavior and interaction. A role perspective is helpful to understand relational, social, and organization structures in that it focuses on the kind of interactions and interdependencies between organizations or organizational units. In the context of project management, the role concept has been applied to the division of labor between project work and the project-client interface. Turner and Keegan (2001) observed that projects typically require two areas of management: internal project management and the management of the external needs and claims by the client. They consequently distinguish the role of the steward and the broker. This confirms role differentiation within project management dealing with different stakeholders (Turner & Keegan, 2001).

An important topic for this research is the potential roles that PMOs take in respect of their stakeholders. One of the most established definitions of a PMO serves as a starting point: "[A PMO is] an organizational body or entity assigned various responsibilities related to the centralized and coordinated management of those projects under its domain. The responsibilities of the PMO can range from providing project management support functions to actually being responsible for the direct management of a project" (Project Management Institute [PMI], 2008, p. 443). This definition has two important implications: first, the concept of the PMO covers a wide range of organizational designs, competences, and interdependencies with the rest of an organization; second, the authority of a PMO may range from a mere "support function" to the actual responsibility "for the direct management of projects" (see quote). The present report contends that the operations of a PMO as a service unit or a management unit it makes a difference in the nature of the inter-PMO relationships and in organizational outcomes. The following is a description of the three basic PMO roles identified:

- **Serving.** PMOs exert a serving role if they operate as a service unit to internal and external units, project managers, and project team members. Typically, a PMO offers a number of support functions to projects or other PMOs to increase resource efficiency and outcome effectiveness. In a serving role, a PMO, for example, could extend the administrative capacity of a project or provide operational support in projects through training, consulting, and providing project management services, or by specialized task execution. It responds to stakeholder needs and ensures overall project or organizational performance.
- **Controlling.** At the other end of the asymmetry, PMOs take on a controlling role when they operate as management units for projects under their domain. Depending on the scope of their managerial authority, they may be responsible for the enforcement of project management standards, such as methods and tools, for the control of compliance with set standards, for evaluation of project performance, and sometimes even for the assessment of employee performance and career promotion. Whenever PMOs are entitled not only to monitor and evaluate but also to take managerial action and sanction malpractice, they exert a role of relative dominance and surveillance over project managers and project team members.
- **Partnering.** A third role, not particularly acknowledged in PMO research is the partnering role. The partnering dimension has received limited or no attention so far and is not explicitly acknowledged in the seminal PMI definition (PMI, 2008). Partnering refers to a relationship, which is characterized by reciprocity, mutuality, and equality. Partnering implies lateral communication between a PMO and other—equally qualified or equally commissioned—PMOs, project managers, or project team members. Such a *coequal* relationship would enable or emerge from cooperation and mutual interdependencies. More concretely, a PMO takes on a partnering role when it engages in equal level knowledge sharing, exchange of expertise, lateral advice giving, and joint learning with equal level stakeholders.

These three PMO roles are presented here as pure theoretical roles. However, in organizational reality, it is more likely that PMOs conduct a mix of the three roles, albeit at different levels of intensity.

2.2.3 Organizational Learning: A Community of Practice Approach

The present research aims at providing in depth understanding of community of PMOs. Is existence of networks with and around PMOs sufficient to claim that a community of PMOs exists? To answer this question, this section turns to community of practices theory as a foundation to build a conceptual framework for communities of PMOs.

Community of practice definition. A *community* (Community, n.d.) defines a group of people with common characteristics or interests living together within a larger society, while *practice* (Practice, n.d.) is defined as the continuous exercise of a profession. The community of practice theory was introduced as a theory of learning from studies of apprenticeship. The initial thoughts on communities of practices have emerged from a profound questioning on the learning process that is the object of the seminal book from Lave and Wenger (1991). These authors proposed the concept of situated learning as a legitimate peripheral participation within a theoretical perspective of social practice, which includes learning. "We are, then, trying to furnish the social world in a way that begins to do justice to the structured forms and relations in which legitimate peripheral participation takes place. Relational, historical conceptions have emerged from this exercise, and this decentering tendency in characteristic of the means we have explored for grasping *person, activity, knowing*, and the *social world*[2]" (Lave & Wenger, 1991, p. 122). The person is considered as a practitioner both involved as a member of a community and as an agent of activity. The person dynamically progresses (as do the community) from a newcomer becoming an old-timer leading to what can be seen as a contradiction between achieving continuity for the community of practice on one hand and the replacement of old-timers. Within the situated learning activity, transformed in legitimated peripheral participation, newcomers move in a centripetal direction under their motivation to become full practitioners. Knowing is part of the social reality where participation is a way of learning. It takes the form of relations "among practitioners, their practices, the artifacts of that practice, and the social organization and political economy of community of practice" (Lave & Wenger, 1991, p. 122).

Wenger and Snyder (2000) defined a community of practice as "groups of people informally bound together by shared expertise and passion for a joined enterprise" (p. 139). Communities of practice are now entering the virtual mode making use of open communication technology such as wikis, webinars, blogs, etc. For example, PMI recently launched multiple communities of practices through its website (www.PMI.org).

Yet, community of practice is anchored in learning. It adopts an integrative constructivist epistemology where different types of knowledge (tacit, explicit, individual, team/organizational) are seen as inseparable and mutually enabling (Bredillet, 2004). "Thus knowledge can be seen as an input of knowing, and knowing as an aspect of our interaction with the social and physical world, and therefore the dynamic interaction of knowledge and knowing can generate new knowledge and new ways of knowing" (Bredillet, 2004, p. 1114). It is opposed to the more traditional positivist epistemology that assumes knowledge is something people have.

Community of practice and other types of groups. Distinction between different types of groups is proposed by Wenger and Snyder (2000, p. 142). The PMO's community of practice is distinct from a formal work group from which specific outcomes are expected, from a project team from which deliverables are expected within a specific budget and period of time, and, lastly, distinct from an informal network formed loosely between employees that share some common interest. While this grouping is useful to distinguish between different groups encountered within the organization, it misses major learning fundamentals based upon the community of practice theory. Bredillet (2004) suggested a typology to distinguish community of practice and project team based specifically on the learning experience. Following Bredillet (2004), members within a community of practice "learn by participating in the community and practicing their jobs" (p. 1130). Conversely, in a project team, "members practice their jobs and learn by participating in the project team.

---

[2] Italics in this citation were marked with an apostrophe in the original text.

A project team is a place where knowledge is created, where members learn knowledge that is embedded, and where knowledge is utilized" (p. 1130). Knowledge occurs in a project team as well as within a community of practice.

Community of practice is an emergent concept and multiple forms are found in reality. Scarbrough and Swan (2008) argued for accepting diversity in the forms a community of practice. They see the concept of community of practice as denoting not a discrete social grouping but rather historically specific expressions of the self-reinforcing relationships between learning, identity, group formation, and social practices. They have shown that project team and community of practice represent different sources of learning and that they overlap, reinforce, and sometimes conflict, depending on the relation between project work and existing social practices.

Managerial paradox. However, precisely, with the wide diffusion of the concept comes a sort of distortion of the initial thoughts (Duguid, 2008a; Lave, 2008). Duguid (2008a) pointed out that community of practice is now an instrument of management: "We also get a theory that appeals strongly not only to business schools, but also to management consultants: it is instrumental, operational, and promises only beneficial results" (p. 7). The initial thoughts on learning as improvisation and autonomy are forgotten and replaced with just the contrary, to follow the rules and avoid any improvisation (Lave & Wenger, 1991; Wenger & Snyder, 2000). Duguid (2008a) saw in this managerial approach to the community of practice the traditional but still strongly alive of the Taylorism: "The community of practice was rapidly domesticated" (p. 7). Nevertheless, Duguid (2008a) and Lave (2008) both admitted that, as any other construct, this one is following its own itinerary.

An example of managerial domestication of community of practice is given within Wenger and Snyder (2000). They promoted communities of practice as a managerial new instrument to reach business results such as helping to drive strategy, starting new lines of business, etc. They defined communities of practice as fundamentally informal and self-organizing and at the same time, they benefit from cultivation. For these authors, cultivation refers to support communities of practice and sustain them over time. This is where the management paradox comes in: on the one side there is the emerging and self-organizing inherent character of community of practice and on the other side, there is the managerial involvement in developing them and integrating them into the organization. In this context, up to what point is a community of practice not becoming a formal working group?

One other dimension of this paradox relates to the knowing *what* and knowing *how*. In community of practice theory, codification of knowing *what* in explicit artifact is possible. Explicit artifacts in project management could be methodology, templates, intranet, and others. However, the knowing *how* needs some kind of a practice to make it actionable (Duguid, 2008b). This paradox often takes the form of best practices diffusion. Best practices refer to explicit knowledge that can be transferred from one organization to the next. But, what is critical in knowledge is not that much the *what* but the *how*, "[. . .] the explicit is worth relatively little" (Duguid, 2008b, p. 81). To solve this paradox, best practices should be re-embedded within the community. This means that best practices go through appropriateness to the community of practices. This appropriateness can lead to adaptation of a best practice to the specific context of the community of practices. In doing so, the community develops and shares the knowing *how*.

In conclusion, it appears that forming a network (as described in section 2.2.2) does not suffice for a community of practices alone. Networks would be better referred to as the underlying structures, which give rise to possible communities of practice. A conceptualization of PMOs as communities of practices is presented in section 2.4.

2.3 Managing Multiple PMOs: The Governance Challenge

The coexistence of multiple PMOs in an organization calls for governance of them in terms of setting their objectives, providing the means to achieve these objectives, and assessing progress (Müller, 2009; Organization for Economic Co-operation and development [OCDE], 2004). The distributed nature of roles and responsibilities in multiple PMO settings adds to the complexity of the governance task. From an organization theory perspective, organizational development resembles the *time-paced evolution in relentlessly shifting organizations,* as described by Brown and Eisenhardt (1997). This theory migrates the well-established theories of punctuated equilibrium into the dynamics of today's organizations and their markets using the structural and communication approaches of successful companies. Results from this research show that successful organizations use neither extremely mechanistic nor extremely organic structures, but adapt their structures to the projects' needs, combined with intensive communication across projects (also shown by Turner & Müller, 2004). The theoretical lens taken in the present study is that of Brown and Eisenhardt (1997), where organizations continuously change and so do their structures—PMO networks develop in order to effectively and efficiently balance the changing needs for project management governance within corporations. The question arises how the network of PMOs that makes up the community of PMOs is governed in this continuously changing organization. This is addressed in the following by looking at network governance as a foundation to support learning in PMO communities.

2.3.1 Governance of Projects

Governance in the context of project management aims for a consistent and predictable delivery of projects' planned contributions to the achievement of the corporations' strategic objectives, done within the framework of corporate governance. Governance defines the structures, roles, responsibilities, relationships, and reporting mechanisms that support the collaboration of the projects and their governance institutions (e.g., PMOs) (Müller, 2009, 2011).

Research in governance of projects and project-based organizations started in 1999 with the identification of different organizational structures, and it is contingent on project size and the number of customers in an organization (Turner & Keegan, 2001). Subsequent research identified specific roles in governance of customer delivery projects, described as the Broker and Stewart model (Turner & Keegan, 2001). The relationship between governance type in terms of project, program, or portfolio orientation of the organization, and its success was researched by Blomquist and Müller (2006), showing significantly higher success for organizations governed by balancing program and portfolio management, than for those focusing their governance on either of the multi-project, program or portfolio management approaches. No research has been conducted yet on the governance of PMOs and their networks.

Attempts to standardize governance at the operational level of organizations started in the IT industry with the COBIT Auditing Standard for IT Centers and later the ITIL standard (Information Systems & Control, 1998). These standards are developed for the operational part of IT organizations.

Contrary to the standardized approaches in operations, Miller and Hobbs (2005) showed that approaches to the governance of projects vary. They identified higher dynamics in governance structures for large capital mega-projects and more network relationships than in binary buyer-seller projects. Research by Klakegg, Williams, Magnussen, and Glasspool (2008) identified *top-down* versus *bottom-up* approaches to the governance of projects, depending on national culture and history of their project management approaches. Here, the former approaches focus on project outcomes, define the accountabilities of the board members, and do not define the processes or tasks of governance (Association for Project Management [APM], 2004). The latter *bottom-up* approaches are add-ons to existing project management methodologies, like PRINCE 2 (Office of Government Commerce [OGC], 2005) and define the processes and tasks in the governance of government procurement projects (OGC, 2009). Other research in governance focused more on industry and project type, mainly with the aim of understanding the particular governance structures for the following:

- Olympics projects (Clegg, Pitsis, Rura-Polley, & Marosszeky, 2002);
- Large capital projects (Miller & Hobbs, 2005);
- NASA projects (Shenhar et al., 2005);
- Construction projects (Pryke, 2005); and
- Public projects (Klakegg et al., 2008).

Classic work by Ouchi and his colleagues showed that organizations govern their control structures by either focusing on process compliance or outcome of work (Ouchi, 1977, 1978; Ouchi & Maguire, 1975). This was later extended by Brown and Eisenhardt (1997) who showed in their case studies that process-oriented project management approaches (i.e., those prioritizing process over project outcome) are associated with less successful organizations, whereas outcome-oriented approaches are associated with the more successful organizations. By linking this concept with the shareholder versus stakeholder orientation of the organizations (i.e., its corporate governance approach (Clarke, 2004)), four different project governance paradigms were identified, which explain the contingency between corporate governance and control of projects (see Table 2-1) (Müller, 2009, 2011).

- The *Conformist* paradigm ensures strict compliance with existing processes, rules, and policies in an attempt to ensure lowest project costs in environments with a relatively homogeneous set of projects. Here tactical PMOs implement one particular project management methodology within the organization.
- The *Flexible economist* paradigm aims for low project costs through a well-informed selection of project management methodologies that ensure economic delivery by only marginally compromising other success criteria. PMOs working in these environments build a range of skills and a toolbox for project managers to use.

Table 2-1. The Four Paradigms in Project Governance

Control Focus		Organizational Governance	
		Shareholder Orientation	Stakeholder Orientation
	Outcome	Flexible Economist	Versatile Artist
	Behavior	Conformist	Agile Pragmatist

- Under the *Versatile artist* paradigm, the benefits are maximized by balancing the diverse set of requirements arising from a number of different stakeholders. PMOs support project managers in the development of new or tailoring of existing methodologies, processes, or tools to balance the diversity of requirements.
- Organizations subscribing to the *Agile pragmatist* paradigm maximize usability and business value of a project's product, through a time-phased approach to product release of functionality over a period of time. These projects often use agile/Scrum methods, with the sponsor prioritizing deliverables by business value over a given timeframe. These organizations rarely have PMOs, but if so, they perform tactical process improvement activities (Müller, 2009).

Governance paradigms may differ by business units or departments within larger companies and are contingent on the idiosyncrasies of the different organization's that make up the company. Examples include projects in marketing or R&D departments, which are often controlled by heir outcome. This is often contrary to maintenance departments, where projects are controlled for their compliance with exiting processes and policies. Communities of PMOs can thereby be made up of PMOs with very different charters. Depending on the project governance paradigm prevalent in the organization the PMO community pursues different objectives, such as instilling process compliance in behavior controlled organizations and flexibility in approaches in outcome-oriented organizations. This may serve as a starting point to investigate the current move from control-oriented PMOs to project-outcome and results-oriented PMOs, and the roles of PMO networks in this type of project governance structures.

From a theoretical perspective, governance is typically explained through transaction costs economics (TCE) (Williamson, 1985), and agency theory (Jensen & Meckling, 1976), where the former addresses the economics of governance and the latter the information balance between governing and governed institutions.

TCE aims for minimizing administrative costs in relational contracting by adapting the governance structures to the idiosyncratic combination of asset specificity (i.e., the uniqueness of the outcome in a transaction), the general uncertainty of the transaction, and the frequency of similar transaction. For example, the higher asset specificity and transaction uncertainty, the more governance is needed (e.g., in terms of contract negotiation and follow-up, control structures administrative efforts) and thus the higher the transaction costs (Williamson, 1975, 1985).

Agency theory implies an information imbalance between the governing and the governed parties, because the governed party knows more about the project/transaction at hand than the governing party does. If both parties want to maximize their utility within the transaction/project then there is a likelihood of conflict and opportunism from one party at the expense of the other. Overcoming this requires careful contracting to align the interest of governing and governed institutions, as well as additional control structures, which increase governance costs (Jensen, 2000; Jensen & Meckling, 1976).

Contemporary approaches align these two theories with project settings by integrating TCE with agency theory and control theory to balance economic, information and control objectives (Müller, 2011), or introduce institutional theory in the form of legitimacy as third dimension to TCE and agency theory especially to govern social and moral acceptance of project activities (Müller, 2009).

2.3.2 Governance of Multi-PMO Structures

TCE and Agency Theory help to explain governance in hierarchical or market-oriented structures. However, they only partly explain the governance of networks of organizations, such as PMOs. With the present study's focus on the company's internal multi-PMOs structure, the hierarchical and network structures are of interest.

Hierarchies and networks are two distinct forms of organization, which require different governance approaches (Provan & Kenis, 2008). Hierarchical structures are typically referred to as built on dyadic relationships in relatively formal and bureaucratic settings. Contrarily, network structures imply more than two actors in complex patterns of interdependencies, typically based on organic and social relationships (Rank, Robins, & Pattison, 2010). The following addresses this difference.

Hierarchical Structures

Hierarchical structures allow for more control over the members and tend to be more bureaucratic. In these cases, they are referred to as mechanistic structures, which are generally less flexible than organic structures (Burns & Stalker, 1994). Mechanistic structures lend themselves to high values in these three organizational properties of the following:

- *Differentiation* (as opposed to integration): This addresses the breaking up of work into distinct tasks and functional subunits and their embeddedness in the organizational hierarchy. High differentiation is often associated with clearly identifiable organizational entities and their specialization. On the contrary, integration calls for more mixed and cross-functional work and decision making.

- *Formalization* (as opposed to organicity): This addresses the extent rules and procedures are explicitly given, typically in writing, to increase efficiency in routine tasks and rational control. This is often related to bureaucracy. Organicity calls for more mutual adjustment and dynamic adaptiveness of actors in the organization.
- *Centralization* (as opposed to decentralization): This addresses the extent decisions are made at the top of the organization's hierarchy. Decentralization refers hereby to decision making at the lower levels of the organization's hierarchy.

The level of centralization, differentiation, and formalization decreases from mechanistic to organic or structures (McPhee & Poole, 2000).

Network Structures

By integrating TCE with social network theory, Jones, Hesterly, and Borgatti (1997) extended existing governance theory to networks. They defined the social mechanisms that resolve exchange problems of adaptation, coordination, and safeguarding in intra-network exchanges between actors. For that, they identified four conditions that define the level of structural embeddedness of transactions in networks, which then enables four social mechanisms for coordinating and safeguarding exchanges in networks. Hereby a particular combination of the four conditions of demand uncertainty with stable supply (i.e., unknown demand for knowledge), highly customized exchanges from experts, complex tasks under time pressure, and frequent exchanges among parties defines the need for network governance and the level of structural embeddedness. High embeddedness implies a larger number of connections that actors have within the network and the freedom to use them as needed. This embeddedness enables social exchange mechanism. In network settings, these social exchange mechanisms replace the traditional governance mechanisms of authority, bureaucratic rules, standardization, or legal recourse. These social mechanisms address the two governance objectives of (Jones et al., 1997):

- *Reducing coordination costs* by restricting access in exchanges to a relevant number of actors, and by building a macroculture, for example, through the use of common language to convey complex information or specifying shared and tacit rules of behavior; and
- *Safeguarding exchanges* by establishing collective sanctions for those who do not obey the macroculture and by being sensitive to the reputations of the network members by spreading information about behavior among parties.

This explains the conditions and the mechanisms for governing exchanges in networks, but not yet how governance is done in networks.

Provan and Kenis (2008) took this understanding a step further by looking at the forms of network governance and their effectiveness. They distinguished networks from other organizational structures by defining networks as being comprised of autonomous entities while simultaneously being goal directed, and therefore as "essentially cooperative endeavors" (p. 231). Their governance requires the use of networked "institutions and structures of authority and collaboration to allocate resources and to coordinate and control joint action across the network as a whole" (p. 231). They identified three forms of network governance: shared governance, a lead organization, or network administrator organization.

Shared Network Governance

Hereby governance is executed inside the network, that is, the members of the network. This can be done in formal or informal ways of interaction. This form of governance relies on the involvement and commitment of either all, or a significant subset of the network members, who are themselves responsible for managing internal and external relationships and coordination. Commitment is hereby built through equality of the members, thus a symmetrical power distribution. This fosters the collectivity of partners, which is needed for joint decisions and management of network activities. While not all governance activities are necessarily performed through all members, the network appears to act collectively. This form of network governance is most effective in networks with few members with high levels of mutual trust, high consensus about the goals the network wants to achieve, and little need for competences in coordinating the network in order to achieve its goals.

Lead Organization-Governed Networks

In this governance form, one actor assumes the leader position. This can be, for example, because of its power or authority or the central position of the actor in terms of resource or knowledge flow. It can also emerge from the members themselves if seen as an effective and efficient way to govern the network, or it may be mandated from outside, for example, through funding organizations. Hereby are all major network activities and key decisions coordinated through the leading actor and are therefore centralized. This form of governance is most effective in networks of moderate size and high levels of trust in the lead organization, as well as moderate levels of consensus about the network's goals and competences in coordinating the network.

Network Administrative Organization

Hereby a separate external organization is set up to govern the network. This organization is not a member of the network and does not provide services within the network. However, it coordinates and governs the network members, their relationships, and activities. The Network Administrative Organization may be appropriate to reduce the complexities of internal governance stemming from shared or lead-organization governance. The existence of a Network Administrative Organization may be justified, for example, through its reputation or mandated by sponsors or higher management. This form of governance is most effective in moderate to large networks (in terms of participants) when the Network Administration Organization is well trusted, moderate goal consensus prevails, and the need for competences in coordinating the network is high.

The governance theories discussed earlier explain to some extent the dynamics seen in constantly changing organizations, such as those described by Brown and Eisenhardt (1997). However, the relation with multi-PMO structures has not yet been investigated.

This section provided a short review of governance of projects and networks. Both perspectives are the supporting ground for governance of multi-PMO settings, which are, in turn, the foundation of learning in PMO communities. To that end, the project governance paradigm shows the fundamental values of the organization when doing its projects. Within this paradigm, the PMOs organize themselves, for example, in the form of hierarchies or networks. These then are the basis for knowledge exchange within the PMO and the wider project management community.

2.4 Conceptualization of Communities of PMOs

This section aims at providing a conceptual framework that integrates concepts to answer the research question: "How to describe communities of PMOs?" (see section 1.1). The conceptual framework builds on the three themes covered in the literature review (sections 2.1 to 2.3).

2.4.1 Definition of Community of PMOs

The concept of community of PMOs is based upon the community of practice concept where both terms, community, and practices, are articulated together to make learning happen in situations. It presupposes that relationships exist between PMOs, and it requires essential community of practices characteristics. The following definition is suggested for community of PMOs:

> A community of PMOs is a network of PMOs formally or informally bound together by shared values and expertise for a joined enterprise.

Obviously, network and relationships are at the foundation of a community of PMOs. PMOs relate to each other within formal or informal settings. Formal settings refer to the ones that are dictate and compulsory within the organization, while informal settings are spontaneous and on a voluntary basis. PMOs' informal relationships respect the pure definition of communities of practices. However, taking only informal relationships would exclude an organizational reality of managerial initiatives aimed at building shared values and expertise. Authors acknowledged and adopted the managerial domestication of the concept of community of practice (Wenger, 2000) to define community of PMOs. The final part of the definition suggests a common practical goal for the members of this community in using the term enterprise. This common goal, the definition suggests, develops around shared values and expertise. In communities of PMOs, the common goal would develop around project management knowledge depending on each particular PMO's mandate. Situated learning happens in the one or the other PMO's functions. In short, community of PMOs is recognizable by the identification of a network of PMOs bound together toward a common practical goal. They can be identified through learning mechanisms where explicit artifacts (knowing *what*) are produced in action (knowing *how*).

From the literature review (see section 2.1), individual PMOs within organizations support the circulation of knowledge. However, as of now, there is no conceptualization on how PMOs relate to each other to create and share project management knowledge other than what is explicitly codified. This research explores for the first time, from our current knowledge, a multi-PMOs situation.

To better understand this phenomenon, the authors propose a conceptual framework that builds on three basic components: social world, governance, and structure of relationships (see Figure 2-3).

2.4.2 Social World of Community of PMOs

Social world is a fundamental component of community of practices theory (Lave & Wenger, 1991). Community of PMOs is also part of a social world, which, in this particular case, resides in an organization. In this research, the unit of analysis is the relationships between

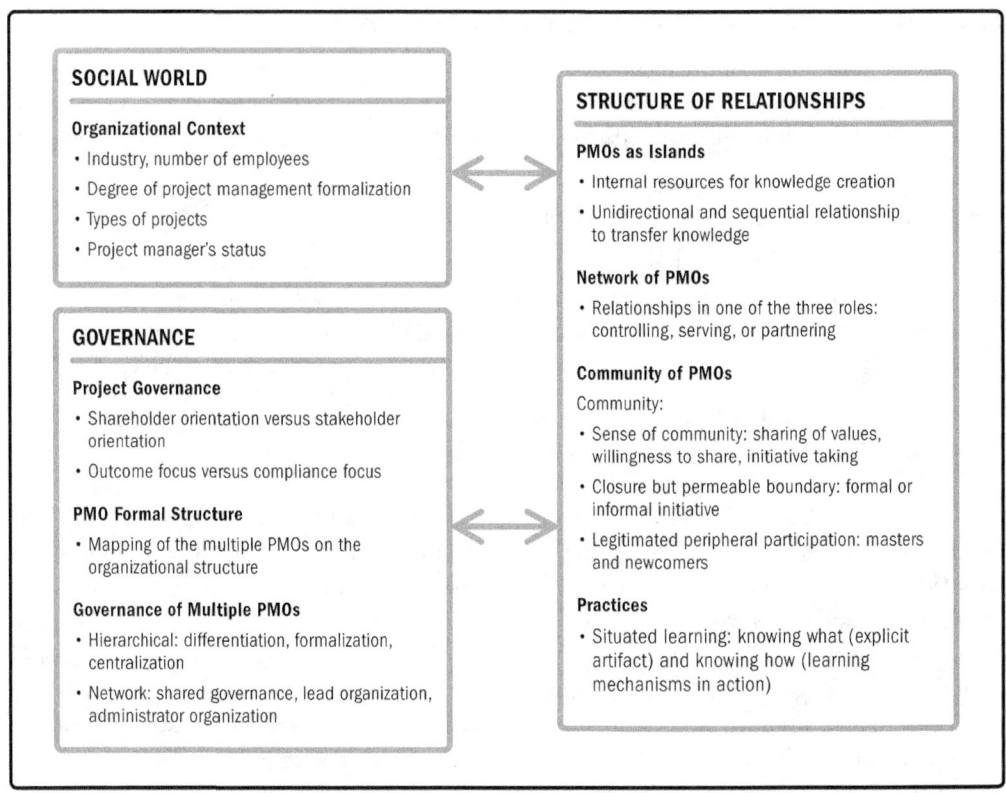

SOCIAL WORLD

Organizational Context
- Industry, number of employees
- Degree of project management formalization
- Types of projects
- Project manager's status

GOVERNANCE

Project Governance
- Shareholder orientation versus stakeholder orientation
- Outcome focus versus compliance focus

PMO Formal Structure
- Mapping of the multiple PMOs on the organizational structure

Governance of Multiple PMOs
- Hierarchical: differentiation, formalization, centralization
- Network: shared governance, lead organization, administrator organization

STRUCTURE OF RELATIONSHIPS

PMOs as Islands
- Internal resources for knowledge creation
- Unidirectional and sequential relationship to transfer knowledge

Network of PMOs
- Relationships in one of the three roles: controlling, serving, or partnering

Community of PMOs
Community:
- Sense of community: sharing of values, willingness to share, initiative taking
- Closure but permeable boundary: formal or informal initiative
- Legitimated peripheral participation: masters and newcomers

Practices
- Situated learning: knowing what (explicit artifact) and knowing how (learning mechanisms in action)

Figure 2-3. Conceptual Framework for Community of PMOs

PMOs. Yet, the PMO's social world in which these relationships happen is described under organizational context. Description of social world could be much more comprehensive but, given the scope of this research, it is limited to the most relevant organizational element regarding the management of projects. Moreover, the governance concept complements to a certain degree the social world context. The organizational context provides relevant information to situate PMOs within their specific environment. It is acknowledged that projects and programs are not isolated islands and that the context within which they are developed and implanted is of primary importance (Engwall, 2003; Pellegrinelli, Partington, Hemington, Mohdzain, & Shah, 2007). The same applies when different types of tensions and issues lead to frequent transformations of PMOs (Aubry et al., 2011). Organizational context plays a major role in the overall understanding of many organizational phenomena (Hughes, 1987).

2.4.3 Governance

In organizations, governance provides fundamental orientation and focus toward all activities. Given the objective of this research, project and multi-PMO governance will contribute to the social world description. This concept contains three complementary dimensions of governance: project governance, PMO formal structure, and governance of multiple PMOs. Governance of projects is described following the model proposed by Müller (2009) and the governance of multi-PMO structures is described through the network governance theory of Provan and Kenis (2008).

The PMOs' formal structure is the mapping of PMOs on the organization chart. When multiple PMOs coexist within one organization, they may be situated at any hierarchical level and can be found in a variety of business or functional units. This approach has the advantage of drawing a clear representation of all PMOs in the specific organizational context, showing each PMO with its relative position regarding the number of layers and the object of projects being business or function.

The multi-PMO structures are described by their structural properties of differentiation, formalization, and specialization, following McPhee and Poole (2000).

2.4.4 Structure of Relationships Between PMOs

The foundation of knowledge management, and eventually of a PMO's community, is the existence of relationships between PMOs. It does not suffice to state that relationships exist between PMOs, but certain types of relationships are more likely to engage people into knowledge sharing and then forming a community of PMOs. Not all groups of PMOs form a community. Three types of relationships are proposed to distinguish between these settings: island, network, and communities of PMOs. The island type of relationship is more likely to develop new knowledge internally and only then will establish temporary relationships to deliver or transfer knowledge (Glückler, 2011). The network of PMOs describes the relationships between PMOs (as shown in section 2.3) and their three basic roles as suggested in the section on network (see section 2.2.2): controlling, serving, and partnering.

From the community of PMOs' concept as defined (see section 2.2.3), two components—community and practices—are articulated together to make learning happen in situations. On the community part, characteristics relate to the sense of community, the boundary around the community of PMOs and the legitimated peripheral participation. On the practices part, situated learning can be observed through mechanisms where explicit artifacts of learning can be identified as well as actions to get these artifacts.

2.4.5 Linking Social World and Governance to the Structure of Relationships

As shown in Figure 2-3, concepts are linked together showing a dynamic interaction between them. Social world and governance may influence the types of relationships PMOs can engage in, and conversely, relationships may shape the social world and eventually the governance mechanisms.

Chapter 3

Research Design and Methodology

This chapter describes the research methodology. It starts by stating the authors' philosophical perspective and then describes the research design and the methods used. This is followed by a description of the qualitative study, the interviews, and their analysis. Subsequently it describes quantitative study, its questionnaire development, the related data collection, and the social network analysis (SNA).

The aim of this study is to understand the nature of PMO communities, their relationships in PMO networks, and the associated governance structures. The reality of a single PMO is quite well known. However, little is actually known when considering multiple PMOs and their relationships. The authors used different methods to understand the different levels of PMOs, their networks, the governance of these networks, and the community of PMO practitioners. The design of this mixed-method approach followed the suggestions of Saunders, Lewis, and Thornhill (2007), who recommend a series of decisions to develop a robust research methodology. This starts with a decision on the philosophy underlying the research. Once that is established, the methodological decisions regarding inductive versus deductive approaches, research strategy, method choices, time horizons, techniques, and procedures can be addressed. The next section describes the choices made for this study.

3.1 Underlying Philosophy

Research philosophy addresses basic questions of how we make sense and analyze the nature of things and relations (i.e., ontology) and the question of how can we create knowledge (i.e., epistemology) (Kilduff, Mehra, & Dunn, 2011). A wide variety of different philosophical stances exists and, they must be combined with methodological choices within a research study. Different combinations of these philosophical stances with particular methodological approaches have proven to be successful in answering different types of research questions and developing theories. Over time, these combinations aspired to the level of research paradigm. Biedenbach and Müller (2011) showed the importance of outlining underlying philosophies and paradigms in research reports. They outlined how research results (which are obtained at the study's end) cannot be interpreted when the study's underlying philosophy (which is determined at the study's start) is not known. Examples include questions like: Are the study's results about one individual or the average of several individuals? Are the results generalizable to a population? Were they obtained to understand the particularities of one organization?

Among the most popular research paradigms are positivism, critical realism, and post-modernism. Here the first is borrowed from the natural sciences and focuses on the empirical association between observable variables for assessing causal relationships using statistical techniques. The second paradigm, realism, also assumes that reality is underpinned by an objective and empirically measurable world of causal effects, but that humans' interpretation of these effects are subjective. Realist researchers are therefore looking into the relationships of unobservable effects, which are "on top" of an objective and observable ground. The third paradigm, postmodernism, focuses on uncovering subversive and underlying power relations and the associated multilayered processes (Bechara & Van de Ven, 2011).

The present study takes a critical realism perspective as described above (Archer, Bhaskar, Collier, Lawson, & Norrie, 1998; Bhaskar, 1975; Sayer, 2000). An abductive approach was used for knowledge development. This was done by reflecting on practical phenomena using, but not limited to, existing knowledge, thus linking own perspectives, theory, and practice for the understanding of real world phenomena. "Such reflection, in fact, is one way that practical knowledge becomes refined and extended into practice wisdom" (Van de Ven & Johnson, 2006, p. 807).

The research questions together with the chosen methodology call for an explorative study using a case study approach (Eisenhardt, 1989). To that end the study does not aim for generalizable results, but for an in-depth understanding of the four cases, which then allows for understanding of the phenomenon of PMO communities in the particular context of the four studied cases. Using multiple cases, the authors were able to synthesize the findings and identify patterns. These patterns might be hypothesized as being of general nature and tested in future studies.

3.2 Research Design

A holistic multi-case research design using a single unit of analysis was used (Yin, 2009) together with sequential mixed method approaches (Tashakkori & Teddie, 1998, 2010) in each case. Case studies are superior research approaches for answering *How* and *Why* type research questions about contemporary events, because they allow for in-depth investigation of a contemporary phenomenon in its context (Yin, 2009). Four case studies were done in this research; each of them was hereby treated as an idiosyncratic expression of the phenomenon under study. The aim was to understand the particularities of the phenomenon *PMO networks* and show how these particularities relate to their context, such as the company within which a PMO network resides. This was done through within-case analysis. By use of replication logic, that is, several case studies for the same research, we were able to analyze the commonalities and differences across cases using cross case synthesis (Yin, 2009).

A combination of inductive and deductive approaches was used for the design of the qualitative and quantitative studies, respectively. A combination of both—an abductive approach—was used for developing the research findings, and the PMO models shown in Chapter 5. The first research method in each case company was qualitative and investigated PMOs and their networks within their context (Patton, 2002). Initial investigations of new phenomena, like this one, are best done using inductive approaches to understand how individuals subjectively assign meaning to the phenomena and interpret them (Eisenhardt &

Graebner, 2007). The authors started with a series of interviews in each case to understand the organizational structure, authority, roles, and responsibilities, as well as the interaction of the different PMOs in their network. Here the authors collected qualitative data to build a holistic picture of each case.

Phenomena for which theory exists in general but not for the particular context for PMO networks, such as knowledge flows, were deductively assessed. This was done as a second method to assess the information flows within PMO networks. The authors objectively assessed the information flows and used quantitative data and analysis techniques to test hypothesized causalities. This step involved the development and use of a questionnaire within two of the case companies. Statistical methods like social network analysis (SNA) were hereby used to identify communication networks and clusters, as well as information flows within and across clusters.

3.3 Case Sampling

A purposive sampling approach to achieve representativeness and comparability was used, which is appropriate "when the researcher wants to (a) select a purposive sample that represents a broader group of cases as closely as possible or (b) set up comparisons among different types of cases" (Teddlie & Yu, 2007, p. 80). Each case is hereby regarded as representative for its particular combination of economic sector and geography, which are:

- A global telecommunications provider in Northern Europe
- A national health care organization in North America
- A European financial institution
- A pharmaceutical manufacturing company in China

Four organizations contributed to this research. These organizations combined some homogeneity and heterogeneity in their characteristics leading to a strong research design (Eisenhardt, 1989). While each organization is specific, all four organizations also share some commonalities: they are large and they have formalized their project management processes through implementation of more than one PMO. Two of the cases are operating in relatively stable markets, while the telecom and pharmaceutical industries are classified as hypercompetitive (Biedenbach & Söderholm, 2008). Table 3-1 shows the characteristics of each case. Fictitious names have been given to the four organizations for their anonymity.

Table 3-1. Case Sampling

	Case 1	Case 2	Case 3	Case 4
Economic Sector	Telecommunications	Healthcare	Finance	Pharmaceutical
Region	Europe	North America	Europe	Asia
Financial Structure	Private	Public	Mutual	Private
Market	Hypercompetitive	Public System Submit to High-Level Cost Pressures	Mature Market	Hypercompetitive

3.4 The Qualitative Study

3.4.1 Data Collection Strategy

To collect appropriate data on our research questions about *how* and *why* organizations work, we followed Yin's (2009) suggestions and selected the organization as a unit of analysis and used individuals as our data sources (see Table 3-2).

The details of the case companies, along with the analyses findings, are presented in Chapter 4.

3.4.2 Interviewee Sampling

The sampling of interviewees per case was done to represent the organizational structure in each case company in the best possible way. One to three interviewees were targeted for each PMO to represent, when possible, a variety of positions. These are the positions: PMO director, manager to whom the PMO director reported, and a PMO employee or an individual working closely with the PMO. The authors' personal contacts helped identify a first PMO interviewee for the targeted positions. This person identified the other targeted interviewees.

Case 1: Global telecommunications provider headquartered in Northern Europe

This global case company is hierarchically structured, with about 500 members in about 200 PMOs worldwide. The hierarchy has two PMOs at the global level (one for development and another for deployment), about two dozen regional PMOs and the rest are country level PMOs. Seven PMOs were investigated. Interviewees included one from each of the two global PMOs, two from regional PMOs (Scandinavia and South East Europe), and three from country level PMOs in Europe. All interviewees had many years of project management experience. Except for the global PMO members, the interviewees were engaged in combinations of supervisor roles at the regional level, managing customer delivery projects at

Table 3-2. Design Versus Data Collection and Unit of Analysis (Adapted from Yin, 2009, p. 89)

		Data Source	
		Individual	Individual
Unit of Analysis	Individual	Individual behavior Individual attitudes Individual perceptions	Individual employee records Interview with individual's supervisor; other employees
	Organization	How organizations work Why organizations work	Personnel policies Organization outcomes

regional or country level, or in consulting junior project managers in their customer delivery projects. Interviewees from the global PMO were senior managers of the organization.

Case 2: Health care service provider in North America

This public health care provider forms a hierarchical structure of multiple quasi-autonomous organizations at three levels: national, regional, and local. At the national level, three PMOs existed and they were all investigated with two interviewees for each of them, PMO executive, the PMO director, and a PMO employee. At the regional level, there are 18 PMOs of various sizes and mandates. From these, four were investigated, one of which has a particular mandate of cumulating both regional and local roles. Nine interviews were conducted with at least one interviewee, in a position varying from executives, PMO director, and project managers within PMO. At the local level, exact total number of PMOs is difficult to find, as there exist hundreds of health care organizations spread over the 95 local centers. Their size varies from small long stay centers to major university hospitals. For this research, targeted organizations were university hospitals in which PMOs existed. Four PMOs were investigated with six interviews with at least the PMO director position and, when possible, with a PMO employee.

Case 3: A European financial institution

This organization maintains a loosely coupled network of four PMOs, of which one is perceived as the "roof" organization in respect to the others. This PMO reports to the board of directors and its mandate is project portfolio management. The other three PMOs are specialized in strategically linking IT with business, planning, and estimating of IT projects, and strategic project development at the national level. Interviewed were the managers of all four PMOs plus at least one member of the PMO organization.

Case 4: Pharmaceutical manufacturing company in China

This company maintains a network of five PMOs. It is made up of five functional managers and directors of five different line organizations (e.g., quality assurance, operations, etc). Each of these managers represents a PMO in his or her line organization. At the corporate level, these five managers form a corporate level PMO. The head of the corporate PMO reports to the CEO of the firm. Ten interviews were held, including the head of the PMO, the PMO members/the functional managers), as well as the vice president of production, project managers, and one administrative person who supports the PMO.

All interviews lasted between 30 and 90 minutes. Forty-seven semi-structured interviews were conducted (see Table 3-3).

Table 3-3. Case Studies Interviews

	Case 1 Telecommunications	Case 2 Healthcare	Case 3 Finance	Case 4 Pharmaceutical	TOTAL
Number of PMOs Investigated	7	11	4	5	**27**
Number of Interviews	7	21	9	10	**47**

3.4.3 Interview Questions

Targeted companies and subsequently the targeted interviewees were approached using the Interview Brief as shown in Appendix A. This was complemented by a phone call, which explained the nature and the purpose of the research. Following the interviewees consent to participate, the researchers conducted the interviews in the facilities of the interviewee.

Within the interviews, data were collected on the case companies' projects, PMO characteristics, PMO communities, PMO employees, and the related governance structures. Appendix B shows the interview guide, which served as a basis for the semi-structured approach to interviewing.

3.4.4 Validity and Reliability of the Interview Data

Validity and reliability of the data were pursued by following Yin (2009). Multiple sources of evidence and supporting evidence were sought (e.g., presentations and reports). Key informants were used, with whom the correctness of data and validation of results were done through subsequent meetings and results workshops. Reliability was assured through pattern finding and replication logic. Table 3-4 shows the approaches taken for the different types of validity and reliability.

3.4.5 Interview Analysis

Interview data were analyzed by using different and complementary strategies (Langley, 1999). The interviews done in the health care case followed a grounded-theory approach in line with the Glaser and Strauss school (Glaser & Strauss, 1967). This implies an analysis after each individual interview and a continuous comparison approach to identify commonalities of the data and their meaning, as well as ruling-out one-time events, thus ensur-

Table 3-4. Approaches to Validity and Reliability of the Interview Data (After Yin, 2009)

Tests	Tactic	Phase	Approach Undertaken
Construct Validity	Use Multiple Sources of Evidence	Data Collection	• Interviews were used to ask for examples, presentations, reports, and other supporting evidence.
	Have Key Informants Review Draft Case Study Report	Composition	• Workshops were held in the case of the pharmaceutical manufacturer and the financial institution. Final reports were drafted for all cases and reviewed by the key informants.
Internal Validity	Do Pattern-Matching	Data Analysis	• Data analysis was done using Miles and Huberman's (1994) iterative process for data collection, data display, data reduction, and conclusion finding. Patterns were identified and matched across cases. • Data were cross-validated between respondents.
External Validity	Use Replication Logic in Multiple-Case Studies	Research Design	• Four case studies were done. Each underwent a within-case analysis. Subsequently, a cross-case analysis was done to synthesize across cases and identify commonalities and differences.
Reliability	Use Case Study Protocol	Data Collection	• A case study protocol was developed at the beginning and used during all data collection efforts.

ing a robust theory. Interviews in this case study were registered and transcribed. Atlas. ti software (ATLAS.ti Software Development, 2004) was used to support the analysis and automate some of the analysis functions.

Interviews in the three other case studies were recorded and notes were taken simultaneously by the researcher. The data were promptly analyzed after the interviews. Analysis followed Miles and Huberman's (1994) iterative cycle of data collection, data display, data reduction, and conclusion finding. In two cases, this led to follow-on interviews to collect more evidence.

Reports were written for each case and handed over to the contact person for review by key informants. The pharmaceutical and finance case study workshops were held with management and key interviewees to present and validate the findings, as well as to suggest some improvements. In the telecommunications case study, the final report was sent to the contact person and validated by him through email. All findings were validated by the case companies.

Cross-case synthesis was undertaken, following Yin (2009) to identify commonalities and differences across the cases. Commonalities were looked for to find those concepts that might have potential to be later hypothesized as of general nature, and therefore testable in a future research. Concepts that were not common across the cases were analyzed for their potential to be context specific. The abductive approach allowed for a steady back and forth between data from the cases and their identified concepts and showed how they relate to each other across the cases. This ensured consistency and validity of the identified concepts. The results of the cross-case synthesis were modeled and, they are further described in Chapter 5.

3.5 The Quantitative Study

In addition to qualitative fieldwork, the research design comprises a social network perspective to study not only the nature and meaning but also the structure of relations between project managers and PMOs. Following the central research question, this mixed-methodology approach proves appropriate to analyze PMO interactions as processes of networks or even communities.

3.5.1 Social Network Analysis

The basic approach of social network analysis (SNA) is to construct topological networks from the complex reality of social relationships and to analyze the positions and roles of individual people or organizations as well as the overall structure of linkages within the network. Generally, a social network "is a specific set of linkages among a defined set of persons, with the additional property that the characteristics of these linkages as a whole may be used to interpret the social behavior of the persons involved" (Mitchell, 1969, p. 2). This definition has at least two implications: first, the principal unit of analysis is the relation rather than the individual actor. Social network theory seeks insights about the constraints and opportunities for individual as wells as collective actors that arise from the relations between them. Second, the specific structure of the overall network as a whole is considered as a condition for these constraints and opportunities. This methodology uses relational information about the interaction between actors, projects and organizations to assess the specific structures and social opportunities that these structures convey (for a detailed introduction, see Scott [2000] or Wasserman and Faust [1994].

Within organization science, methods of social network analysis have been increasingly applied to studies of knowledge management and knowledge transfer within large organizations (Glückler, 2008, 2011; Reagans & McEvily, 2003; Tsai, 2001), informal governance (Lazega, 2000, 2001), and the geography of innovation (Almeida & Kogut, 1999; Breschi & Lissoni, 2009; Powell, Koput, & Smith-Doerr, 1996; Sorenson & Waguespack, 2006). There have also been some recent applications of social network analysis to the research field of project management (Brookes, Morton, Dainty, & Burns, 2006; Mead, 2001; Pryke & Pearson, 2006). However, to our knowledge, no research has so far made use of this methodology for the analysis of the highly interwoven webs of project management offices. It is a central tenet of this study that a more profound examination of the relational structures of projects, project managers, and PMOs in large organizations will benefit from the application of SNA.

3.5.2 Data Collection

Network data are often used from secondary sources such as statistical data sources (e.g., trade statistics between national or regional economies or patent statistics between inventors and patent applicants), or other databanks that contain or permit the construction of relational data (e.g., digital protocols on communication flows through email, telephone etc.). The advantage of these data is that they usually convey complete data for the entire network and thus avoid the problem of missing observations. The downside of these data are that for many research questions in the social sciences, communication records over telephone or email are insufficient representations of the quality of the relationship between any two actors (Glückler, 2010). For many research questions, secondary data often fail to provide the necessary validity and reliability of observations. For instance, what do email traffic statistics reveal about the content of the interaction and the nature of the social relationship? Since the focus of this research is on interpersonal knowledge flow between people in an organization, this flow of knowledge has to be assessed through primary observations. Therefore, the empirical research strategy focuses on a network survey.

However, the collection of primary network data in the field is a complex and challenging task (Glückler, 2010; Ter Wal & Boschma, 2009) because surveys usually fail to produce complete information. In the empirical analysis of networks, missing linkages cannot be compensated by estimation. Every single relation is unpredictable information that influences the overall network structure. Discrepancies between an observed and the 'real' network cannot be calculated (Schnell, Hill, & Esser, 1995). Under conditions of imperfect data, it has been shown that the correlation between real and observed measures of most centrality measures converges to 1 with increasing size of the sample. When the sample covers 70 percent or more of the population, the correlation coefficients for almost all measures are 0.8 or higher (Costenbader & Valente, 2003). Largely, network measures of centrality are relatively robust against random network disruptions and imperfect data (Borgatti & Carley, 2006). Therefore, a high response rate is a limiting factor with respect to both the quality of analysis and the necessary effort and cost to be taken by the target organization. This risk is intrinsic to the method and therefore makes it difficult to collect primary network data at the same rate of participation as, for instance, interviews or classical surveys. In this research, all four case studies were analyzed by means of social network analysis yet with varying degrees of intensity. In three cases, interviews and other documents were used to construct network representations of the interactions between the numerous PMOs in each respective organization. These network graphical representations are used for visual interpretation, and they support the interpretations within the mixed-method approach.

In one case study (Pharma), the organization agreed to participate entirely in an organization-wide survey on the relationships and interpersonal knowledge transfer between all employees in project management and in the PMOs. The survey took place in early 2010 and elicited responses from 89 employees. The extraordinary response rate of 99 percent was the result of a very professional survey management and the commitment and support by the PMO executive management in the respective organization. This nearly complete dataset thus offers a unique and first time opportunity to analyze the structure of interaction in and between project management offices.

3.5.3 Questionnaire Development

The social network questionnaire consists of two parts (cf. Appendix C). While the first part covers information about the characteristics, opinions, and assessments of the individual respondents, the second part captures the linkages between a focal respondent and all other respondents in the organization.

The first part of the questionnaire comprises 22 questions that address three groups of items.

Characteristics of the respondent such as age, area, and degree of education, languages spoken, position in the organization, business function, office location, years of employment with the organization, area of expertise, number of projects worked on, and number of projects as project manager.

Individual statements about the value of knowledge transfer with other colleagues, the overall performance of the PMOs at the organization, the contribution of PMOs to individual knowledge transfer, and the individual contribution of the respondent to knowledge transfer.

Individual suggestions for the improvement of knowledge transfer in the organization.

The second part of the questionnaire comprises two relational questions that capture the individual relationships between the employees with respect to the interpersonal exchange of knowledge. The two questions are constructed as redundant on purpose to duplicate the central question of who provides/receives knowledge to/from whom (cf. reliability of data):

- "Please list as many people as you consider important inside the company for providing you with expertise related to project management. Please check twice that you have not forgotten anyone from whom you received relevant PM knowledge."
- "Within this firm, who are the persons that have provided significant expertise to help you solve project management-related problems over the last years?"

3.5.4 Validity and Reliability of the Data

Networks are always social constructions by the researcher. First, real networks are usually unlimited because any individual is connected to many other individuals in some way. It is therefore impossible to identify complete empirical networks. Second, relationships are usually characterized by a degree of multiplicity, i.e., a mixture of various kinds of relations. Colleagues may exchange work-related knowledge and be friends or even relatives at the same time. Often, one would expect one layer of meaning to affect the other layers. The definition of a size (here: project managers and PMO members in an organization) and of an explicit quality of relation (here: interpersonal knowledge transfer) are necessary operations for the analysis of social network structures. Empirical networks are always socially constructed analytical reductions based on conceptual criteria (Marsden, 1990, p. 439).

The validity of the data in the network survey was controlled through repeated prior interviews about the nature of work and the nature of knowledge requests that employees face in their environment. Once the questionnaire was designed, the items were discussed with the PMO executive and pretested with representatives of the organization. As a result, the individual items were found understandable, interpretable, and appropriate indicators for the intended observations of knowledge flows.

The reliability of the network data is often a challenge because people usually tend not to recall all contacts that are relevant for a certain issue (Marsden, 2003). This research controlled for potential recall errors by means of the cross-validation method (Krackhardt, 1990; Hansen, 2002). If a respondent indicated that he or she had provided knowledge to a colleague, the survey also collected the information of that colleague whether he or she had received that knowledge from the former. The empirical analysis is only based on exclusively those linkages that are confirmed by the sender and the receiver of work-related knowledge.

In sum, the network survey conveyed valid and reliable data on the structure of inter-personal knowledge transfer in and between PMOs because measures and items were checked and found appropriate by representatives of the organization, because the response was nearly complete (99 percent), and because only cross-validated data were considered for analysis.

Chapter 4

Descriptions of Case Studies

As presented in the chapter on methodology, case studies were undertaken to provide in depth understanding on governance and communities of PMOs. As shown in the conceptual framework Figure 2-3, data were collected to populate the three major concepts: social world, governance, and structure of the relationships between PMOs. This chapter briefly describes the four case studies aiming to provide the necessary information to the reader to follow the logical line that leads to research findings and their interpretation. The following information is provided for each case study:

- Context: Complementary to the description of the industry context in section 3.3, this section focuses on project management context, i.e., formalization of project management, type of projects, and project manager status.
- Project governance: As suggested in the conceptual framework (see Figure 2-3), projects evolve in a particular project governance paradigm that helps or refrain knowledge flow between PMOs. Descriptions of project governance are provided through the governance model diagram (see Table 2-1).
- PMOs formal structure: The multiple PMOs within large organizations can be represented as a hierarchical or network structure usually mirroring the organizational structure. However, contrary to the hierarchy, the PMOs' formal structure is not always a reporting structure. In this section, PMOs' formal structure is described (1) by the identification of the PMOs' position in this structure; and (2) by their structural properties: differentiation, formalization, and centralization.
- Governance of multiple PMOs: this element is central to answer the question if PMOs are working together or not. Each PMO or level of PMOs is scrutinized to identify if relationships exist between other PMOs or levels of PMOs. When such relationships exist, they are described as a hierarchy of PMOs (differentiation, formalization, centralization) or a network of PMOs (shared governance, lead organization, administrator organization).
- Communities of PMOs: Not all networks of PMOs form a community. Learning mechanisms involving a PMO have been identified. They are classified in relation with the hierarchical position a PMO occupied within the formal structure. The object of knowledge and the type of knowledge (explicit or implicit) are identified for each learning mechanism.
- Each case study description concludes with a table summarizing major descriptive elements. A global cross-cases analysis of the four case studies is presented at the end of the chapter.

4.1 Case Study 1: Telecommunications Provider

4.1.1 Context

This case company is a long established global provider of telecommunication networks, telecom services, and multimedia solutions. The company (hereafter called Telecom) employs about 40,000 professionals and is headquartered in Europe. Projects at Telecom are systems integration, multimedia, or network rollout. The majority of projects are delivery projects to a wide variety of external customers in approximately 170 countries.

Project management is seen as a core competence and is well established in the organization. Project managers are formally assigned to projects and respected in this position. Most of the project managers are professionally certified.

PMOs have been part of Telecom for more than a decade. Most interviewees indicated that there were several PMOs before the current one, with the current one being in existence for about three to four years. The particular role of the current PMO network is to provide subject matter expertise (SME) in project management for the country organizations and the project management practitioners. This can be through deployment of corporate project management methods, consulting, and coaching of practitioners, but also through provision of project management services within those countries where this expertise is not (yet) built-up or only needed for a few projects. Standard methodologies are used for project management and project governance. Project performance is assessed along the lines of reaching targets for time, budgets, quality, and customer satisfaction.

PMO employees are mainly (50 percent to 80 percent) certified project managers, who are well trained, experienced and mentored. Experience typically increases with the level of the PMO. At the headquarters level, PMO members are described as having more than 10 years of experience, often in customer-facing projects, but also from other parts of the organization.

4.1.2 Project Governance

The governance of projects at Telecom is very much aligned with its corporate governance. Policies are in place for processes, career paths, methodology, business processes, etc. At times, they are felt as being too rigid by the practitioners. Projects are classified by their complexity from A to D (A = simple) and different processes are used contingent on complexity level.

Telecom is a customer delivery organization with emphasis on customer satisfaction. At times, this is in conflict with the strong process and compliance orientation of headquarters. The question whether project governance is more shareholder or more stakeholder driven shows mixed results (see Figure 4-1). Most interviewees referred to an "in-between" status of finding the right balance, where project managers are expected to be good corporate citizens and adjust their shareholder or stakeholder orientation to the situation at hand. A similar pattern emerges on the question whether control is more at the level of outcomes or at the level of compliance (behavior). All interviewees referred to the importance of clear processes and the expectance of compliance with it. However, in the interest of business and customer-related outcomes, the process may be sacrificed. Interestingly, the headquarters groups' opinions are to the contrary. They see Telecom as a process-oriented global organization.

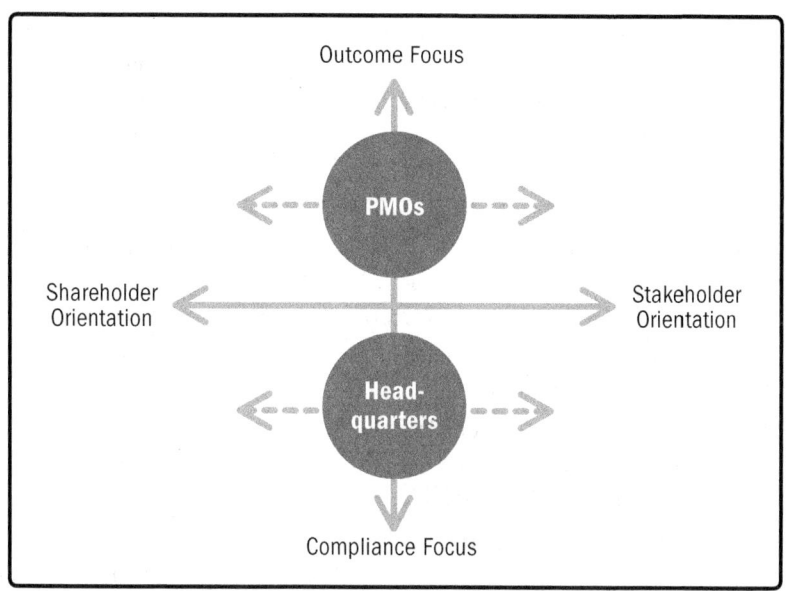

Figure 4-1. Project Governance Paradigm at Telecom

4.1.3 PMOs' Formal Structure

Telecom-wide, there are approximately 500 people in about 200 PMOs in 24 regions. The PMOs are hierarchically organized at three levels: corporate, regional and country. At the corporate level, there are two PMOs: a Headquarters PMO, which "owns" the project management methodology and service, and a Global PMO, which deploys these developments on a global basis. Regional PMOs support country organizations and deploy there what has been handed over to them by the Global PMO. Country level PMOs are managing the projects in their country.

The tasks and work split between PMOs is coordinated through charters, objectives, and incentives and controlled through key performance indicators (KPIs) at each level in the hierarchy. A hierarchy of charters, objectives, and incentives exists, where those of the Global PMO are broken down to the regional and then to the country level. All lower levels in the hierarchy contribute their particular higher-level subset.

Headquarters PMO. Their charter is to ensure that the Telecom PMO is recognized in the market as a world-class PMO. Headquarters PMO owns and develops the policies, processes, methods, tools, career ladder, and training curricula or certification programs. They provide their deliverables on the corporate intranet for global use, work with internal and external partners for the deployment of project management, and work on project management maturity using a maturity model derived from the Capability Maturity Model Integration (CMMI) from the Software Engineering Institute (SEI) at Carnegie Mellon University (Software Engineering Institute, 2011).

Global PMO. This PMO deploys the developments of the Headquarters PMO, ensures compliance, and measures deployment using KPIs, like achievement of time, cost, quality, and customer satisfaction at the project level. They identify skills gaps by assessing the maturity of the organization, partly through help from external assessors. The gaps are identified through audits and could be related to project management methodology, resource capabilities, PMOs, collecting of compliance data, etc. In addition, their mission is also to provide resources to balance competence lacks globally by providing resources to the regions and countries on an as-needed basis. To that end, the PMO acts similarly to the regional PMO, but acts on a global basis.

Regional PMOs. At the regional level, PMO members are assigned to troubleshooting tasks, such as bringing projects back on track. For that, PMO members work mainly with local project managers in the country organizations. A small group of specialists works in noncustomer facing roles that are mainly for standardization and improvement of project management within the organization.

Country PMOs. At the country level, PMO members are assigned to projects to manage the end-to-end delivery at customer sites. Responsibilities include delivery within time, cost, quality, and customer satisfaction constraints.

The point of differentiation between PMOs is mainly between the operational and centralized headquarters function. Corporate functions differ greatly in their task and are more focused on the development of implementation blueprints and establishing project management within the regions and countries. At the regional clusters level differentiation is relatively low, because these PMOs mainly fulfill similar functions across all clusters. Differentiation at the country level is referred to as being related to the particular mix of contracts by country (e.g., some countries have more roll-outs, others more bespoke solutions). Differentiation between country, region, and global deployment is in the amount of travelling, price and seniority.

4.1.4 Governance of Multiple PMOs

The PMO structure at Telecom is hierarchically organized. Its structural properties of differentiation, formalization and centralization are all high:

- High *differentiation* of tasks across the layers of Headquarters, global, regional and country PMOs.
- High *formalization* of work through existing policies and methods, but also through defined meeting schedules, hierarchically linked charters and objectives.
- High *centralization* of decision making, with the Headquarters PMO taking project management deployment decisions. which are subsequently implemented and partly customized at the lower levels of the hierarchy.

Governance is executed at the top of the hierarchy, thus through the Headquarters PMO by defining the overall structure of the PMO hierarchy, the relationships between the PMO and between PMOs and their regional and country organization.

This relatively strong level of mechanic structure of the hierarchy complements the dynamics of the hypercompetitive market in which the organization belongs. This can be interpreted in different ways, for example:

- The PMO structure appears to provide an "anchor" or "stable equilibrium point" to balance the dynamics of the projects in day-to-day work.

- When interpreted in the context of the project governance paradigm, a discrepancy between Headquarters and customer-oriented PMOs emerge. The Headquarters PMO sees the organization's projects governed by a compliance focus, whereas the other PMOs admit that outcome in front of the customer is more important than process compliance.

Taken these views together, the global, regional, and country PMOs appear to be in a dilemma by having to balance the requirements for compliance from Headquarters and the need for customer satisfaction and appropriate outcome at the customer site. According to the interviewees, PMO members should try to be good citizens and do what they are told, but in the end, customer satisfaction (outcome) takes priority.

4.1.5 Relationships Between PMOs

Relationships between the PMOs are top-down in a formal structure, which is not their main reporting structure. The analysis of PMO's relationships from the controlling, serving, and partnering perspective identifies a dominance of controlling and partnering functions, with serving only done at the regional and country level (see Table 4-1).

The relationships among PMOs are held up through meetings and a web place with databases, forums, threads, etc. The web place has been used for several years. At the operational level, it is often used by PMO members to ask questions to the community of PMOs. These questions can be of almost any nature, like asking for project management expertise or solving project management issues. Further use is in sharing of best practices, meeting headquarters' representatives, having online sessions, or asking a project manager to support a country organization onsite. Coordination of tasks and agreement on work split between PMOs is also

Table 4-1. PMO Roles in Telecom

PMOs Identification and Type	PMO Basic Roles		
	Serving	Controlling	Partnering
1. Headquarters PMO	LOW	HIGH • Development and ownership of project management, its processes, methods, and policies	LOW
2. Global PMO	LOW	HIGH • Worldwide deployment • Evaluation of maturity	MODERATE • Tailoring to regional needs
3. Regional PMO	LOW • Manage projects on behalf of country project manager	MODERATE • Deployment of processes, methods, and policies	HIGH • Recovery of troubled projects • Knowledge transfer to local project managers • Tailoring to local needs
4. Country PMO	HIGH • Managing projects	LOW	LOW

done through this platform, using chat rooms, messages, database entries, and other means. New or updated processes and methodology elements are posed by the Headquarters PMO.

1. *Headquarters PMO.* This PMO is mainly in a controlling function. The layered concept of PMOs is developed here as a blueprint and then handed over to the Global PMO for them to deploy it at the regional and country level, where it is subsequently adapted to local requirements. The Headquarters PMO obtains feedback on the scope and depth of deployment at the regional and country level through the work of the global PMO. This resembles a strong control function of the Headquarters PMO.

   Control is exercised using a balanced score card, where the accomplishments of 15 KPIs are evaluated. An important enabler for much of the collaboration is the communication platform, through which much of the feedback on the methodology, KPIs, compliance data, etc., is received.

2. *Global PMO.* This PMO works as the interface between the Headquarters PMO and the regional PMO by managing global deployment and assessing and evaluating project management maturity in the regions. This indicates a control function in respect to regional PMOs. However, other work is done in partnership with the regional PMOs, for example, the tailoring of the Headquarters PMOs deployment blueprints to the needs of the regions, or in supporting regions in balancing resources across organizational and country borders, as well as organizing an annual global learning event. Here all PMO directors are invited to share their issues and experiences and to listen to presentations given by researchers or professionals from the project management field.

   The Global PMO controls the achievements of the regional PMOs through KPIs.

3. *Regional level PMOs.* Regional level PMOs work mainly in a partnering role with country PMOs, for example, in project recoveries or skills transfer. Some control through standardization and improvement of project management within the organization is also done here. Occasionally, regional PMO members manage projects within a country, which implies a serving function for that particular country PMO.

   Coordination at the regional level is done through resource managers. These are individuals within a regional PMO who handle requests from country PMOs and other organizations and link these requests with regional PMO resources for them to take over and work on the given task.

   At the regional level, monthly teleconferences take place, with contents centering on reporting, training, and sharing of resources.

4. *Country level PMOs.* Country level PMOs are in a serving role. Their members manage projects at customer sites toward set objectives in terms of time, cost, quality, and customer satisfaction, thus they provide project management services to the local country organization and their projects. Monthly face-to-face meetings are held within the country PMO. The head of the country PMO takes part in a monthly teleconference with the Regional PMO.

   Collaboration between the regional and country PMOs typically starts after the pre-sales phase of projects. The country organization owns the contract and if needed, the regional PMOs provide SMEs on request. This can be in the form of a regional project manager supporting a country project manager, or by the regional project manager taking over the project (at least temporarily).

Table 4-2. Telecom Learning Mechanisms

Organizational Level	Learning Mechanisms	Object of Knowledge	Type E: Explicit I: Implicit
Headquarters PMO	Annual event	Best practices, updates	E
	Monthly meeting	State of deployment	E
	Web place	New and updated method elements	E
Global PMO	KPI, balanced scorecard	Performance	E
	Monthly teleconferences Audits, reviews Web place	Work balance	E
		Performance	E
		Best practices	I/E
Regional PMO	Monthly teleconferences	Method updates	I/E
		Resource lacks	I/E
		Performance	E
Country Level	Monthly face-to-face meeting	Best practices	I
	Coaching by regional PMO	Best practices	I

The interactions between PMOs within the Telecommunications case, in terms of PMOs roles, are summarized in Table 4-1.

4.1.6 Learning Mechanisms

A number of learning mechanisms can be found at the different layers in Telecom. They are outlined in Table 4-2. Most of them are of explicit type. Learning mechanisms of implicit type are found at lower level PMOs, regional, and country.

The Telecom case study showed the coexistence of multiple PMO relationships at different degrees of role intensity. Descriptive synthesis of Telecom is presented in Table 4-3.

4.2 Case Study 2: National Health Care Organization

4.2.1 Context

This case study is a public health care service provider constituted of quasi-autonomous organizations spread over three structural layers: national, regional, and local (hereafter referred to as Health Care). In this environment, stakeholders and change management are crucial to succeed. At the national level, projects are information systems or information technology (IS/IT) projects. They are designed and developed to answer the ministry's objectives in terms of health care. Users of these projects are at the local level, more often in hospital or health care centers. Implementation of projects is under the responsibility of the regional level, which has to work closely with the local hospitals or health care centers to implement the technology and to manage the process change with people. At the local level, there are a great variety of smaller projects that responds to particular needs of a clinical department. There is not yet a clear inventory of the total number of projects in the entire health care organization.

Table 4-3. Synthesis of Telecom

Case Descriptive Element		Major Characteristics
Context	Formalization of project management	High degree of formalization
	Types of projects	Most projects are software solutions delivered to telecom operators around the world
	Project managers status	Project managers are respected. Most of them are professionally certified.
Project Governance	Stakeholders vs. shareholders orientation	In between situation between two extremes
	Outcome focus vs. compliance focus	Headquarters PMOs focus on compliance to standards
		Other PMOs focus more strongly on the outcomes from projects
Formal Structure of PMOs	Position within the hierarchy	PMOs are spread over three levels in the organization hierarchy:
		Corporate level: Headquarters PMO and Global PMO
		Region: Regional PMOs
		Country: National PMOs
	Basic statement of the PMO mission	Headquarters: being recognized as a world class PMO
		Global: provider of project management processes, tools, and techniques and provision of resources
		Regional: support project management of project at country level
		Country: direct project management of projects
Governance of Multiple PMOs	Hierarchical structure	Hierarchical and mechanistic structure
		High levels of differentiation, formalization, and centralization
		Governance by Headquarters PMO
Roles	Intensity in the three roles: controlling-serving-partnering	Headquarters: high controlling
		Global: high controlling
		Regional: high partnering
		Country: high serving
Practices	Learning mechanisms	At the corporate level, there are two formal learning mechanisms, both being more or less compulsory.
		Wide varieties of mechanisms coexist, both formal and informal. A significant characteristic is the crucial role of the IT platform to support these mechanisms.

Project management practices are quite well established at the national level but are often limited to the IS/IT sector. There are various roles to PMOs depending on their level and on their leadership to implement and develop project management competencies. Project methodology has been adopted since a few years at the national level and is actually in implementation at the other levels. Since 2004, rigorous governance rules apply to project management of large projects.

In general, project management is not seen as a core competency in the health care case study. All resources are dedicated to caring of the population. Consequently, most of the

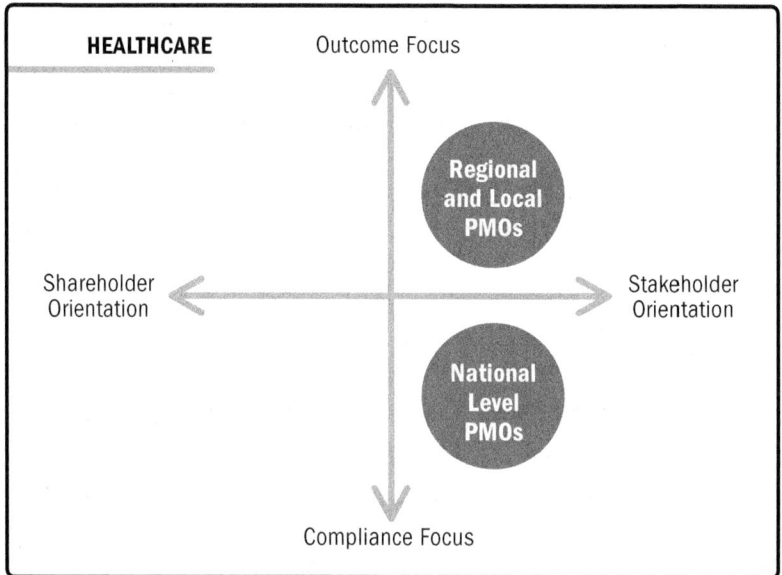

Figure 4-2. Project Governance in Health Care

project managers come from consulting firms; this holds across all levels. At the local level, project management is undertaken by internal employees, usually nurses, without any formal education in project management. Project management tasks add to the day-to-day workload.

4.2.2 Project Governance

In the health care case study, projects are managed in two different paradigms within the stakeholder orientation (see Figure 4-2). The health care case study organization is a public institution and, as such, proprietary interests are diffuse in the society. Many groups can then be involved in public projects and, in particular, in health care projects. Projects have to take into consideration multiple stakeholders needs and expectation in projects. However, tension exists between the outcome focus versus the compliance focus. National PMOs are rather associated with the compliance focus. At this level, there are quite good project management methodologies, processes, and tools. Portfolio management is in place for their projects. They ask for results in terms of their respective budget, schedule, and scope. At the regional and local levels, results are assessed in terms of quality of services to the population. They acknowledge the necessity of rigor in project management, but the outcomes orientation predominates.

4.2.3 PMOs' Formal Structure

The formal structure of the PMOs at the health care case study mirrors the organizational three layers structure: national, regional, and local levels. At the national level, there are three PMOs, 18 at the regional level and more than one hundred at the local level, with various mandates either in local administrative centers, or in local centers of care delivery or in university hospital centers. One PMO is a regional and local PMO simultaneously.

National IT PMO. This PMO is located within the IT department and is primarily responsible for project portfolio management and more specifically, it is concerned with investment strategy, project coordination, and project control. It also aims at enhancing the overall project management competencies by the implementation of project management methodology, tools, and techniques at the regional level. This PMO also manages a *PMO coordination committee* where all regional PMO directors meet on a monthly basis. This committee serves as a sharing and learning mechanism resulting in spreading out best practices to enhance the project management competencies.

Personal Health Record PMO. The second PMO at the national level is dedicated to the specific project of personal health record (PHR).

National IT supplier. The third one is the delivery arm where projects are realized and delivered to their clients. This PMO is a private partner outside the ministry structure.

Regional level PMOs. The 18 regional PMOs have been put in place following a recommendation from the national level. The majority of them are located in the IT department even if projects are rarely purely IT. There are large variations between these 18 PMOs regarding their size and their maturity in project management. These PMOs are accountable for the implementation of the projects in local settings. Their project managers are particularly interested in the implementation strategy and change management. They are experts in IT/IS rather than in project management.

Regional/local PMO. This PMO has a particular double mandate including regional and local responsibilities. Like regional PMOs, it has a strong function dedicated to implementation of major projects at the local centers. In addition, this PMO interacts directly with the local health centers to provide project management services.

Local PMOs. They are located in global local centers or within individual hospitals and health care centers. This level also includes university hospitals. Therefore, they are in direct contact with patients. Approximately one hundred PMOs are distributed across the local health care institutions. Similar variations in size and project management maturity exist between local PMOs. The largest PMOs are actually found in university hospitals, as major investments are put there. PMOs are often specialized in construction, IT, or process reengineering. Project managers are often professionally certified.

University hospital PMO. This PMO is located within a university health care center. The major challenge in its mandate is to support the overall changes in moving from six hospitals to two locations, one of which being a complete new large hospital. In this PMO, there are 10 employees (not consultants), all of them being trained and having experience in project management.

4.2.4 Governance of Multiple PMOs

Within the health care case study, PMOs are structured in two different modes: one mode following more or less the formal hierarchical structure, and the other one forming networks emerging spontaneously depending on specific tasks to be realized and on encounters as they happened. In the hierarchical network, the structural governance properties are these:

- High *differentiation* of tasks across the layers, each one being a quite autonomous entity.

- Low *formalization* of project work when considering the overall network. At the ministry level, formalization is at higher level than everywhere else in the network.
- *Centralization* is very high when controlling the project budget, otherwise *centralization* is rather low.

When taking into account the emerging networks of PMOs, their properties are these:

- High *shared governance* between the participants of the temporary networks.
- Low *lead organization,* as there are relatively small numbers of participants and they are rather self organized.
- Low *administrator organization* for the same reason as the previous item.

In the health care case, it can be observed that multiple governance mechanisms may coexist in the same organization. In the hierarchical network, budget governance is the ministry level accountability. Otherwise, management autonomy leads each PMO to act under the corporate governance where it pertains. In these conditions, it appears difficult to implement any standardization and centralization of project management processes. The emerging PMO networks are more likely within a self-managed governance. The network holds as long as there is a common interest.

4.2.5 Relationships Between PMOs

Relationships between the 11 PMOs that have participated in this research follow the top-down formal structure that is not a reporting structure. The analysis of PMO's relationships under the basic PMO roles (controlling, serving, and partnering) permits to identify five different groups of PMOs that are presented in more detail in the following paragraphs and are summarized in Table 4.4.

1. *National IT PMO and PMO for Personal Health Care Record Project.* These PMOs perform two high level functions for controlling and partnering in relationship with others PMOs. On the one hand, they strongly control projects within strict governance mechanisms. The national IT PMO requests from the local hospital PMO to report periodically on their projects costs expenditures and projections. It asks for financial indictors or for more global value-added indicators. On the other hand, the same PMO initiated knowledge platform that could be associated to the concept of communities of practices. It takes the form of national committees, one grouping regional PMO directors and another one grouping regional project managers. There are monthly face-to-face meetings. The ultimate goal is to develop and to engage the national health care system in project management culture. In the short term, the objective is to share good practices and to develop together any missing processes or tools. The partnering shows less intensive function in the implementation of project portfolio management. Actually, there is no inventory of all projects going on at all three levels in the health care national system and consequently, there is no idea of the global resources allocated to projects. However, regional and local organizations sometimes perceive this initiative as an intrusive approach. The serving function is performed at a very low level.

Table 4-4. PMO Roles in Health Care

PMOs' Role Identification	PMO Basic Roles		
	Serving	Controlling	Partnering
1. National IT PMO and PHR PMO	LOW	HIGH • Monitor and control projects costs/schedule/content particularly with local PMO for major projects and with the National IT supplier PMO.	HIGH • Knowledge national platform with regional PMO directors and project managers. MODERATE • Implementation of project portfolio management: inventory of projects.
2. National IT Supplier and Local PMOs	LOW	HIGH • Develop methodology, processes and tools. • Monitor and control projects costs/schedule/content particularly with major projects subcontractors.	LOW
3. Regional PMOs	HIGH • Develop and implement methodology, provide tools. • Manage projects under their regional mandate. • Provide support to project teams for project not directly in their mandate.	LOW TO MODERATE • Monitoring and control of projects under their mandate.	MODERATE • Participation in the national PMO coordination committee. • To local PMO directors: informal sharing of good practices. Low partnering function: • To internal organizational governance: not that much included.
4. Regional/Local PMO	HIGH • Develop a project management framework, including methodology, processes, and tools. • Manage project in a coaching approach. • Provide support to project teams for project not directly in their mandate.	LOW • PMO: not acting as controller but collect information to present a global view of the project portfolio, soft approach to management language.	HIGH • Participation in the national PMO coordination committee. • With regional and PMO directors: informal sharing of good practices. • Participate and influence internal organizational governance.
5. University Hospital	MODERATE • Clear mandate to support organizational change. • Manage projects: Co-construction with project team. • Innovation is encouraged. • Support project management within a multidisciplinary advisor committee.	MODERATE • To national project governance: provide strict monitoring and control of project. A specific function of the PMO is to evaluate projects and project management financial report.	MODERATE • Executive board members as "partners" to the PMO. • Knowledge acquisition and transfer through projects. • Strong relationship with other functional departments.

2. *National IT Supplier and Local PMOs*. These PMOs concentrate their most important function to the surveillance and do not perform that much of partnering and serving. This function is accompanied with strong project management techniques and strict methodology, processes, and tools. The national IT supplier PMO adopted a strategy of suppliers to deliver IT software components. This PMO manages a portfolio of contracts. With strong project management methodology, processes, and tools, this PMO can monitor and control their suppliers' work. Not surprisingly, this PMO owns an ISO certification in project management. Local PMOs dedicated to IT or real estate projects present similar roles in terms of their relations with other PMOs.

3. *Regional PMOs*. Regional PMOs present a strong function of serving clients and thus are associated with the subordinate type. Everything is turned toward the goal of satisfying the need of their clients. Their mandate covers two types of projects based upon their client: internal client—more often from a functional unit—and local needs where clinical solutions are directly implemented for patients. They manage projects for the former and they support project managers for the latter. Following this serving approach, control of projects is rather low. Considering now the partnering function, PMOs of this type are at a low or moderate level. They are at a low partnering level when considering its role in respect to internal organizational governance. These regional PMOs are only partially involved in governance. However, when taking specifically a project management perspective, these PMOs participate in partnerships at the national level as a member of the PMOs coordination table. These PMOs are also associated with other local or regional PMO directors for sharing experience in an informal approach.

4. *Regional/local PMOs*. Like regional PMOs, this PMO has a strong serving role dedicated to its internal client and to local needs and a quite low controlling role over projects. This PMO has developed its own project management framework that includes methodology, processes, and tools. It has a soft approach with its clients to get them engaged softly in project management. However, this PMO has a strong partnering function. Its director participates very strongly in the national PMOs coordination committee and in other specific working subcommittees. He also created other networks between PMO directors to share and build new components within its project management framework. This PMO participates actively in the internal organizational governance. The project management framework is at a point to be accepted at the organization level as a common project management language.

5. *University Hospital PMO*. This PMO might be quite exceptional showing moderate results in all three dimensions of serving, controlling, and partnering. It refers to a PMO in a university hospital with a mandate to accompany a major organizational change. Serving clients is clearly in its mandate. Generic project methodology processes and tools have been developed but are adapted to each specific project's needs. Innovation in management is encouraged. A multidisciplinary advisory committee has been put in place for the PMO to support the entire organization in project management and ultimately in managing changes. This PMO has also to provide results to the national governance level within strict financial limitations. A specific function within the PMO is to evaluate projects and project management financial performance and to

report on it. Turning now to partnering, this PMO establishes strong internal links. It participates in the executive board where members are considered as partners of the PMO (PMOs has given them the title of partners). Another partnering function relates to knowledge management. This PMO has implemented a specific function to collect and share knowledge through projects and a specific role of knowledge broker. PMO director wants projects to be based upon evidence-based data. This is true for clinical content and for management content. PMO has taken the leadership to establish a strong relationship with other functional departments such as human resources or quality management. A common project management process was developed to insure a common and appropriate contribution from those units to projects.

4.2.6 Learning Mechanisms

Multiple learning mechanisms were found in the Health Care organization. The PMO coordination committee is a central learning mechanisms in this case study for both, the organizer (the National IT PMO) and the participants (regional PMO directors) (see Table 4-5). At the

Table 4-5. Health Care Learning Mechanisms

Organizational Level	Learning Mechanisms	Object of Knowledge	Type E: Explicit I: Implicit
National Level	Organizing and supporting the PMO Coordination Committee	PMO Implementation process	E
		Standardization of processes, tools	E
		Common language in project management	E
		Search for efficiency: not reinventing the wheel	E
		Inventory of projects at regional and local levels (portfolio embryo)	E
Regional Level	Participation to the PMO Coordination Committee	Obtain knowledge on specific methodology	I/E
		Share experience on this methodology and other project management tools and systems	I
	Creation of new networks (outside the Committee)	Sharing on solution	I/E
	Newcomer to the PMO	Experiences by a newcomer of the PMO methodology and tools in order to improve them	E
	Ad hoc meeting	Sharing experiences in PMO management	I
	Action within the PMO mission: to accompany project management	Transfer of knowledge in implementing a PMO	I
Local Level	Formalization of a knowledge broker role	Clinical and management knowledge	E
	Managerial/research team	Management evidence-based practice	E
	Common development of processes (quality, change management)	Processes	E

higher level, all learning mechanisms are of an explicit type, which is contrary to the other two levels.

Table 4-6 summarizes the Health Care case study. It brings together the multiple facets of multiple PMOs environment that were presented in this section.

Table 4-6. Synthesis of Health Care

Case Descriptive Element		Major Characteristics
Context	Formalization of project management	Good degree of formalization at the national level in the IS/IT sector, but rather low elsewhere at regional and local levels.
	Types of projects	Projects mainly deserve clinical and administrative needs. Development of major projects is realized at the national level while their implementation is under the responsibility of regional and local levels.
	Project manager's status	Most project managers are consultants or internal employees without any formal education in project management.
Project Governance	Stakeholders vs. shareholders orientation	Stakeholder orientation
	Outcome focus vs. compliance focus	National level: compliance focus Regional and local: outcome focus
Formal Structure of PMOs	Position within the hierarchy	PMOs are spread over three levels in the organizational hierarchy: National Level: National IT PMO, Personal Health Record PMO, and National IT supplier Regional level: Regional PMOs Regional/local PMO Local level: local PMOs and University hospital PMO
	Basic statement of the PMO mission	National IT PMO: diffuse project management culture through all levels Personal Health Record PMO: idem, but limited to this single major project National IT supplier: provide IT services to Regional PMOs: implement projects in local centers Regional/local PMO: particular case with regional and local mandates Local PMOs: Support project management University hospital PMO: support major change

Governance of Multiple PMOs	Hierarchical structure
	
	Network structure
		Two different PMO networks:
		  1. Hierarchical: high level of differentiation, low level in formalization and centralization
		  2. Emerging networks: low levels of differentiation, formalization and centralization
		Governance by the ministry level, only in respect of budget.

Roles	Intensity in the three roles: controlling-serving-partnering	National IT PMO and PHR PMO: strong in controlling and in partnering National IT supplier and local PMOs: high in controlling Regional PMOs: high in controlling Regional / local PMO: high in serving and partnering University hospital: moderate in all three
Practices	Learning mechanisms	Multiple mechanisms exist. Most of them are under a formal type at the national level, while they are more informal at other levels.

4.3 Case Study 3: Financial Services Provider

4.3.1 Context

This European financial institution (hereafter called Bank) has been part of a large North American bank until it was recently acquired by a European cooperative bank. The Bank has about 335 sales locations in more than 200 cities in their country. The Bank employs around 6,600 employees and provides services to more than 3.4 million customers within the country.

Project management does not appear to be a core competence in the organization. Most of the employees and PMO managers do not have a formal project management education; they were promoted to PMO work based on their extensive experience of working in or with projects. Project management knowledge is conceptualized and standardized in a procedure manual, called Software Development Lifecycle (SDLC), which serves as the guiding principle both for PMOs and for anyone involved in projects.

Projects and project-oriented ways of working are prioritized by management, which is shown by the existence of two project management offices, which report directly to the executive board, parallel with other functional structures. About 100 projects are going on simultaneously at any time. The types of projects are mainly IT-related operational improvement and systems integration projects. These projects stem largely from the recent merger of the two institutions and the need for consolidation of the different IT systems from both institutions.

Processes play a major role in initiation, prioritization, and implementation of projects within the PMOs. Processes are perceived as one of the core competencies of the bank. One of the interviewees stated "Especially in terms of operations, the Bank has the most cost-efficient processes in [the country]."

4.3.2 Project Governance

The majority of projects are internal to the Bank. During the case study, the Bank was undergoing a shift in project governance paradigms. Most of the interviewees mentioned that they were used to the shareholder culture of the prior owner, but with the change in owner, a shift towards a stakeholder approach took place.

Most of the interviewees mentioned that the organization is outcome-oriented. "Though the processes are a strong element of the PMO work, however, we are driving processes for the results," said a PMO manager. There seems to be an implicit prioritization of outcomes over processes within the organization. In addition, the new owner tends to give more space to PMOs for establishing long-term and strategic improvements.

However, as shown in Figure 4-3, a principle difference exists between PMO managers and employees' perception of their projects governance. While PMO managers perceive the governance being outcome oriented, the majority of PMO members perceive the governance being more compliance and process than outcome oriented. The PMO managers' opinion is also different from that of project managers. The process orientation of PMO management is perceived by project managers as overly restrictive. Examples include that the PMO is not informed when project performance gets compromised, even though the process would require it. In these cases, project managers feel the involvement of the PMO as overly

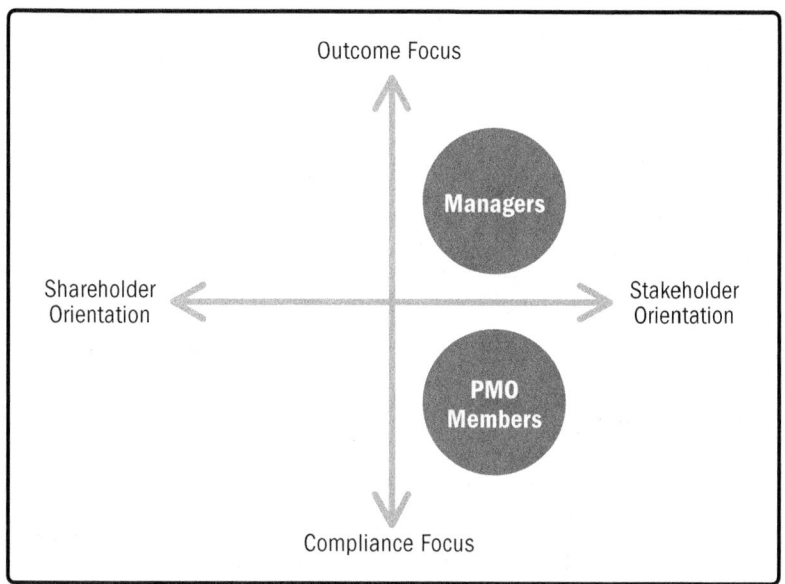

Figure 4-3. Project Governance Paradigm at the Bank

bureaucratic and more of a hindrance than a help. Management is aware of that, but equally unsure about the "value" that the PMO delivers in such cases.

4.3.3 PMOs' Formal Structure

Four PMOs collaborate in a loosely coupled manner, with the business project office being the "roof" organization over the other PMOs. Each of the PMOs addresses different aspects of PMO work, such as:

Business Project Office (BPO). This PMO reports to the executive board. The eight-person PMO is made up of a management group and an expert group for finance, marketing, and strategy projects. The BPO is the roof organization for all PMOs in the Bank. They ensure communication between business and IT; and provide related processes, portfolio management, and follow-up on projects. Their main day-to-day task is portfolio management, that is, selecting, launching, and following-up the "right" projects for the bank.

Project Management and Strategic Integration Office (PMSI). This PMO also reports to the Executive Board, but is functionally a subordinate of BPO. The 20-person PMO focuses on IT projects by translating business requirements into IT requirements; assessing the impact of IT changes on policies, structures, etc, and by testing software.

Local IT Project Office (Local IT PO). This PMO reports to the IT Operations Committee. This six-person PMO coordinates and tracks the largest cross-organizational IT projects. It is led by the Chief Information Officer of the new owner of the Bank.

Strategic Project Office (SPO). This PMO reports to the Operations and Technology (O&T) department. Their focus is on strategic projects in O&T, which can, but must not be IT projects. Their mandate is the development of strategies for the O&T department, as well as management of some of these projects.

The PMO organizations are relatively autonomous and are not linked to each other through vertical lines, but they are subordinate to higher management levels in the organization. However, they are supposed to work on almost the same set of projects.

4.3.4 Governance of the Multiple PMOs

The PMOs are organized in a network. The structural properties of differentiation, formalization, and centralization are all low:

- High *differentiation* of tasks across the BPO and the other PMOs. However, the interfaces of the PMOs' responsibilities are deliberately vague to foster integration of actors for task accomplishment.
- Low *formalization* of work through a focus on informal collaboration to accomplish the organization's objectives.
- Low *centralization* of decision making, by fostering joint decision making among PMOs.

Governance of the PMO network is shared between the PMOs. The requirements of the project or task determine the relationships between PMOs.

This relatively strong level of organic structure of the network complements the relatively stable market that the organization is in. To that end, the PMO network appears to provide flexibility and job enrichment for PMO members to balance the stable day-to-day work with projects. When interpreted in the context of the project governance paradigm, a discrepancy between PMO managers and PMO members emerges. PMO managers see the organization's projects governed by an outcome focus, whereas PMOs members feel to be controlled at the level of process compliance. Interviewees indicated that the BPO is occasionally circumvented when project managers refuse to escalate project performance issues to the BPO in fear of overly bureaucratic audits or reporting "sanctions."

In summary, the BPO has to balance its formal function as a "roof" organization of all PMOs with the loosely coupled and informal network relationships with the other PMOs. The governance function performed by the BPO can thereby be distinguished into formal and informal governance:

- Formal governance through implicit authority as "roof" organization, including defined links with other PMOs and final decision authority; and
- Informal governance through reliance on social interaction, good relationships, and informal communication structures.

4.3.5 Relationships Between PMOs

The PMOs collaborate as a loosely coupled system. Their relationships are both hierarchical as well as at peer level. The BPO has a central role as it provides the overall portfolio view for projects at the Bank-wide level. PMSI and IT PO are limited to IT project portfolio views only, and SPO has solely an O&T perspective. The PMO roles are summarized in Table 4-7.

1. *Business Project Office (BPO).* The BPO is the "roof organization" of all PMOs with a holistic view over all projects. They are in a strong controlling role through their portfolio management and decision making, ownership of the project management process

Table 4-7. PMO Roles in Bank

PMOs Identification	PMO Basic Roles		
	Serving	**Controlling**	**Partnering**
1. Business Office Project (BPO)	LOW	HIGH • Portfolio management of country level projects • Ownership of processes • Project follow-up	LOW
2. Project Management and Strategic Integration Office (PMSI)	MODERATE • Application testing	LOW	HIGH • Interface business and IT through translation of requirements • Assess impact of IT changes
3. Local IT PO	HIGH • Corporate wide IT projects	LOW	LOW
4. Strategic Project Office (SPO)	MODERATE • Project management for some of the strategic projects	LOW	MODERATE • Definition of strategic projects

and their follow-up role on projects. The BPO collaborates closely with PMSI and SPO, contrarily to the Local IT PO, whose working relationship with BPO is less integrated. The Local IT PO reports to the BPO on project status, accomplishments, and issues.

2. *Project Management and Strategic Integration Office (PMSI).* The PMSI's main task is translating business requirements into technical requirements, assessment of impact of changes on policies, structures, etc. In this role, they show a high partnering profile across the IT and business functions of the organization. Serving is done to a moderate extent by testing software, which is developed elsewhere in the organization in accordance with specifications that this PMO helped to translate from business to IT language. The PMSI has very strong links with the Local IT PO for clarifying project requirements and scope. They collaborate with the BPO for project prioritization and "Go/No Go" decisions. PMSI, BPO, and Local IT PO share the same master spreadsheet for projects' status.

3. *Local IT Project Office (Local IT PO).* The Local IT PO focuses on cross-organizational IT projects and coordinates and tracks the largest IT change projects. Doing this they mainly perform a serving role for and within corporate-wide IT projects.

4. *Strategic Project Office (SPO).* The SPO defines the projects for the O&T department in a partnering role. However, the SPO also manages some of these projects, which constitutes a serving role. So their combined role is the most balanced role among all PMOs, given by the balance of a partnering and a serving role in their work.

The SPO and Local IT PO are both within Operations and Technology, but interact relatively little in their project work. SPO mainly interacts with the BPO in resource- and content-based prechecks of initiatives/projects, as well as in estimating and prioritizing for the Bank-wide portfolio to the BPO.

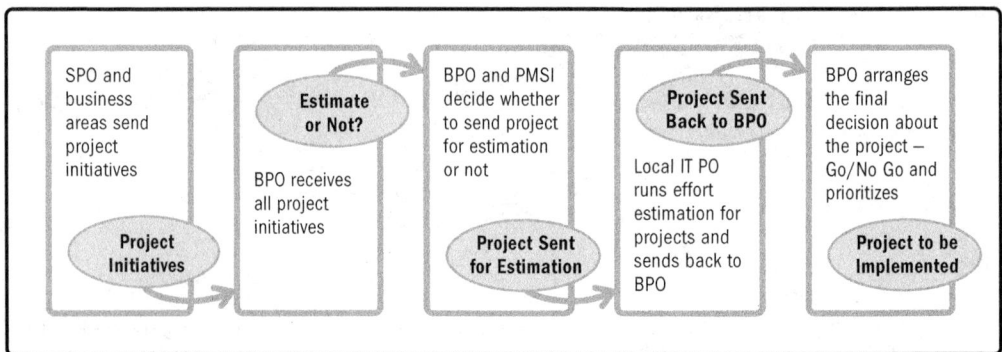

Figure 4-4. Interaction of PMOs Within the Process for Handling Project Requests (after Tsaturyan, 2010)

Interaction among PMOs takes place through a number of scheduled meetings. PMO representatives split responsibilities among each other to synchronize activities. As a central PMO, the BPO coordinates and controls the activities of the other PMOs. However, their interactions are less well defined and are more at an informal and cooperative level. For example, the meetings for the synchronization of control among the PMOs do not have a central coordinating PMO. Managers take on moderator roles in those meetings. They keep track of the meetings, but are not in a formal position or have ascribed responsibilities.

As an example of PMO collaboration, Figure 4-4 shows the process for handling of project requests through the four PMOs.

Intense communication is seen as key in managing the challenges of the loosely coupled PMO network. An underlying assumption is that project difficulties often arise from miscommunication. When new PMOs are established, the initial vagueness and redundancy in responsibilities in respect to other PMOS is solved through meetings. Here the processes and mandates of each PMO are discussed to clarify the borderlines of their responsibilities.

Communication takes place:

- Daily between PMO managers;
- Weekly between management, and PMO internal; and
- Monthly between PMO members (cross PMO).

Interaction between PMOs and projects is mostly through reports and other formalized documentation, as well as the IT platform. PMOs mode of controlling projects is by reporting and updating both upwards and downwards in the organization. In the past, the BPO enforced strongly external control in projects (i.e., reporting and updating of project status) in order to keep track of projects. Because of that, the PMOs met resistance from the project managers in the form of inconsistencies with the formalized processes. Managerial changes and the new owner loosened the level of control exercised by the PMOs over projects.

Table 4-8. Bank Learning Mechanisms

Organizational Level	Learning Mechanisms	Object of Knowledge	Type E: Explicit I: Implicit
Business Process Office (BPO)	Audits, reviews	Best practices, updates	E
	Web place	Updated method elements	E
Business Process Office (BPO) and Project Management and Strategic Integration Office (PMSI) and Local IT PO	Shared spreadsheet	Project status	E

4.3.6 Learning Mechanisms

Very few learning mechanisms can be found in the Bank case study, and all of them are of the explicit type. They are outlined in Table 4-8.

Synthesis of the Bank case is presented in Table 4-9.

4.4 Case Study 4: Pharmaceutical Corporation

4.4.1 Context

This company is a relatively young (16 years old) development and manufacturing company of medical and health care products with headquarters in China (hereafter called Pharma). Since its start-up, the company grew extensively within an established, but competitive market. The majority of its 30,000 people workforce is employed in China. However, cooperation with other institutions and sales is done worldwide.

In recent history, the company went through an organizational transformation from process orientation toward project orientation. Many aspects of day-to-day business, which were perceived as being process or operations in the past, are now approached from a project perspective. This led to project thinking, which is supportive for both the way work is accomplished within Pharma as well as for the project manager community in their daily work for accomplishing project results. This organizational move towards *projectification* contributed to a significant reduction in friction between line and project management.

Project management is well established within Pharma. The majority of the approximately 90 project managers underwent an internal certification program. This program is in scope and breadth comparable to established external certifications, like Project Management Institute's® Project Management Professional (PMP)® credential or the International Project Management Association's (IPMA) Level C certification. However, Pharma's certification program is slightly more focused on the particularities of the pharmaceutical industry and the organization's projects.

Table 4-9. Synthesis of Bank

Case Descriptive Element		Major Characteristics
Context	Formalization of project management	Project management culture is young but standard processes exist throughout the whole organization.
	Types of projects	IT projects mostly for internal clients: operational improvement and systems integration.
	Project manager's status	Most of them do not have formal project management education.
Project Governance	Stakeholders versus shareholders orientation	Stakeholder orientation
	Outcome focus versus compliance focus	PMO managers: outcome focus PMO members and project managers: compliance focus
Formal Structure of PMOs	Loosely coupled network	PMOs are spread over the organization: Corporate level: Business Project Office and Project Management and Strategic Integration Office International IT: Local IT Project Office National: Strategic Project Office
	Basic statement of PMOs' mission	Business Project Office: provide strong portfolio management for the Bank. Project Management and Strategic Integration Office: interface between business and IT. Local IT Project Office: at the top level of IT, it coordinates and tracks cross-organizational IT projects. Strategic Project Office: Development of strategies and management of some of these projects.
Governance of Multiple PMOs	PMO network organization	Organic network structure High level of differentiation, low level of formalization and centralization.
	Network governance	Governance shared across PMOs
Roles	Intensity in the three roles: controlling-serving-partnering	Business Project Office: high controlling
		Project Management and Strategic Integration Office: high partnering.
		Local IT Project Office: high serving
		Strategic Project Office: no one high role; moderate in serving and partnering.
Practices	Learning mechanisms	Most learning mechanisms are formal and it seems that knowledge does not flow easily.

Project managers are formally assigned to projects and respected in this role. Depending on the project type, scope, and importance, project managers are appointed from the ranks of line managers, unit managers, or technical experts. Project managers are consulted when it comes to performance evaluations of project team members.

Projects are typically of shorter duration (less than 1 year) and the majority are operational improvement projects, such as projects for quality improvement or production process improvement. Project managers feel generally that line management supports them in their project management work. However, the support is perceived as being stronger when the project objectives are congruent with line management objectives.

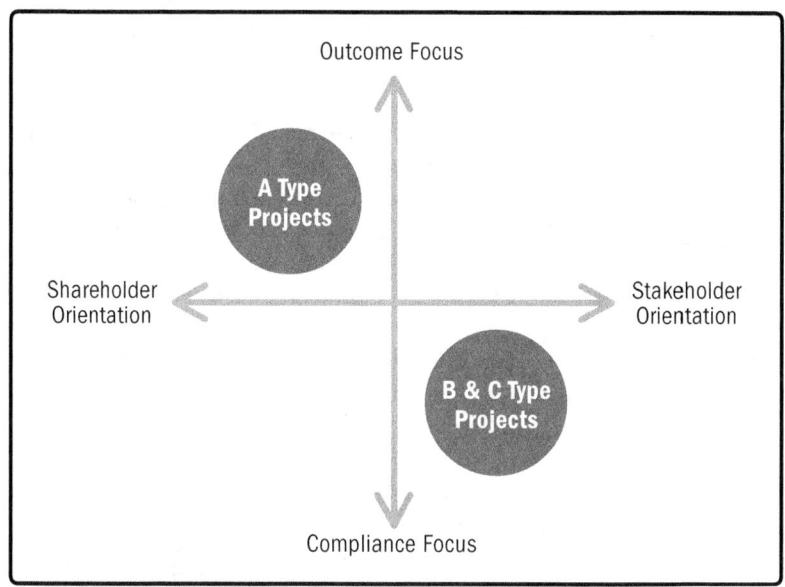

Figure 4-5. Governance Paradigms for Pharma

4.4.2 Project Governance

Projects are categorized into one of these three categories:

- A = company-wide projects, often of strategic value for the organization. These projects are typically managed by the most experienced project managers.
- B = cross departmental, often including some level of cross-department activity, with four to five milestones. These projects are typically managed by experienced, but not the most senior project managers.
- C = within the functional role of a department or organizational entity. These projects are often managed by junior project managers.

Recent months showed a trend away from the A type of projects toward more B and C types of projects. This implies a shift in the required skills profiles toward more junior project managers.

Category A projects tend to be governed by a shareholder orientation and outcome focus, whereas B and C types of projects are governed by a stakeholder orientation combined with process compliance focus (see Figure 4-5). It indicates that strategic projects are aiming for contributions to shareholder return on investment by giving autonomy to project managers for the accomplishment of these goals. Whereby smaller and nonstrategic projects are governed by compliance focus, where less experienced project managers should work in conformance with the PMO established processes and methodology.

4.4.3 PMOs' Formal Structure

The PMO reports to the president of the corporation and consists of two groups:

- A group of five PMO members who are composed of line managers from different departments and different levels in the organizational hierarchy (e.g., directors, department managers, and their deputies). In their line organizations, these managers fulfill a dual role by simultaneously representing a PMO in their organization and maintaining a functional role as director or department manager.

- A full-time information management group is responsible for project and project management related communication in form of information collection and distribution, mainly using an IT platform. This administrative group reports to the Head of the PMO. This group is not investigated in this present study.

There are approximately 90 project managers in the different departments of the organization. Twelve of them are considered as being experts in their particular area of project management. Because of their specific knowledge, they are occasionally asked to consult the PMO group in case of issues related to their respective area of expertise.

Some of the key functions of the PMO include:

- *Definition of practices.* This comprises, among others, the development of methods, processes, and techniques.
- *Authorizing and validating of projects.* The PMO classifies and authorizes projects for execution, and subsequently assesses project success. Authorization is typically done at the beginning of the year and is often based on feasibility studies.
- *Provision of steering committee and escalation functions.* The PMO acts as steering committee for projects and as the institution for escalation of unresolved issues from the projects. The latter is often in the form of providing needed expert resources or other forms of knowledge transfer.
- *Administration of internal certification program for project managers.* This is perceived to be at least equivalent to the popular external project management certifications.
- *Provision of the IT platform for methodology sharing, reporting, and general communication.* The information management group within the PMO provides the infrastructure as well as the up-to-date contents of the project management related information across the organization. Project managers access the project management methods and techniques, as well as report project status and progress through this platform. The PMO members review the information provided.

The PMO sets the context for project management within the organization. To that end, the PMO does not interfere with the project managers' day-to-day work, but governs project management in a subtle and comprehensive manner.

4.4.4 Governance of Multiple PMOs

The PMO network at Pharma is hierarchically organized. Its structural properties of differentiation, formalization, and centralization are medium to high:

- Medium level of *differentiation* of tasks across the organizational layers of PMO and departments. PMO members have a dual responsibility at the departmental and at the corporate level. An expert group at the project manager level is consulted when needed.

- High *formalization* of work through existing policies and methods, but also through the high level of authority of the PMO when it comes to project selection, steering group functions, escalation functions, internal certification, and performance appraisal of project managers.
- High *centralization* of decision making, with the corporate PMO being the decision authority for the development and deployment, but also the governance of project management across the organization.

Governance of PMO is executed at the top of the hierarchy by the Head of the PMO, who works in collaboration with the PMO representatives in the departments.

As in the case of Telecom, a relatively strong mechanistic structure in the PMO hierarchy complements the dynamics of a hypercompetitive market that the organization is in. Again, this can be interpreted as the PMO being an "anchor" or "stable equilibrium point" to balance the dynamics of the projects in day-to-day work. However, contrary to the Telecom case, the understanding of the organizational project governance paradigm appears to be shared across the PMO and the project managers, an effect that might be related to the steering group function of the PMO and other involvements in day-to-day work of project managers.

4.4.5 Relationships Between PMOs

At the corporate level, the PMO selects projects, assigns project managers, and provides the methods, techniques, career path, certification, and communication platform for project managers. At the department level, the PMO functions as the steering committee and the escalation point for projects in execution. Both levels resemble a high controlling role. To a smaller extent, the PMO provides training to project managers, which indicates a partnering role, albeit in the context of the wider controlling role. Table 4.10 summarizes the roles and functions of the corporate and department level PMO in this case.

Table 4-10. PMO Roles in Pharma

PMOs Identification and Type	PMO Basic Roles		
	Serving	Controlling	Partnering
1. Corporate level PMO	LOW	HIGH • Authorizing of projects • Ownership of processes, methods and policies • Project steering group • Evaluation of project and project manager performance • Certification program	LOW • Knowledge transfer through training
2. Department level PMO		HIGH • Deployment of project management	

The PMO members coordinate their previously mentioned activities in a monthly face-to-face meeting. Furthermore, they plan and facilitate knowledge management activities as described in the following.

The PMO members collaborate tightly. They jointly classify projects as either A, B, or C and authorize them for execution. This categorization is a composite of several measures of project scope, complexity, and importance. Finished projects are assessed by the PMO members by evaluating the process, which was used for the project, the business impact in terms of, for example, marketing, sales, finance, process improvement, quality, or safety. Other success criteria, like project costs, quality, resource utilization, etc., are assessed by the parent (line) organization of the project and they complement the assessment of the PMO.

Developments by the PMO (e.g., related to methodology or certification program) are done in collaboration with the project management experts from the line organizations. For that, an individual PMO member takes on responsibility for development and subsequently assembles a team to work on accomplishing the task. The results are reviewed by the other PMO members and the selected expert from the expert group. Accepted new developments are then handed over to the information management team to disseminate the information and provide the newly developed product or service to the project managers using the IT platform.

4.4.6 Learning Mechanisms

Table 4-11 shows the different learning mechanisms applied by the PMO and the knowledge objects that are addressed during these events. Project portfolio composition is communicated at authorization meetings, whereas formal methodological items are provided through the IT platform. Practices are trained and assessed in the internal certification program, while their application is addressed in face-to-face settings, like Steering Group or Community of Practice meetings. In this case study, almost all learning mechanisms are explicit.

Table 4-12 summarizes the attributes of the Pharma case.

Table 4-11. Pharma Learning Mechanisms

Organizational Level	Learning Mechanisms	Object of Knowledge	Type E: Explicit I: Implicit
Corporate	Methodology development	Processes, tools, and techniques	E
	Project authorization meetings	Portfolio of projects	E
	Internal certification	General and specific practices	E
	Project manager's community of practices meeting	Practices	I/E
Department	Audits		E
	Project reviews		E
	Steering group functions		E

Table 4-12. Synthesis of Pharma

Case Descriptive Element		Major Characteristics
Context	Formalization of project management	Project management is well established throughout the company
	Types of projects	Most projects are operational improvements but they vary in terms of scope and complexity
	Project managers' status	All project managers are respected and for the majority internally certified
Project Governance	Stakeholders versus shareholders orientation	Strategic projects (type A): shareholder orientation Other projects: (type B and C): stakeholder orientation
	Outcome focus versus compliance focus	Strategic projects (type A): outcome focus Other projects: (type B and C): compliance focus
Formal Structure of PMOs	Position within the hierarchy	Headquarters PMO, representatives in five key line organizations
	Basic statement of PMOs mission	Projectification of the company
Governance of Multiple PMOs	Hierarchical structure	Hierarchical and mechanistic structure Medium levels of differentiation, high levels of formalization and centralization Governance by head of organization
Roles	Intensity in the three roles: controlling-serving-partnering	Corporate PMO: controlling
		Department PMO: controlling
Practices	Learning mechanisms	Multiple mechanisms initiated from the corporate virtual PMO, most of them being of explicit type.

4.5 Cross-Case Synthesis

Cross-case synthesis takes into account the richness of the data collected on the phenomenon and its context. In this study, the cross-case synthesis was done using a meta-matrix for the grouping of all major characteristics from the four cases (see Table 4-13). For this purpose, major characteristics were linked to the initial conceptual framework (see Figure 2-3). By way of this, the present section provides a first level of descriptive synthesis between the four cases. Specific in-depth cross-cases synthesis on PMO roles is provided in Chapter 5.

As mentioned in Chapter 3, the four case studies presented similarities and differences that help synthesizing the characteristics of multiple PMOs.

4.5.1 Social World

The social world of PMOs is wide and complex. Only a subset of the real social world experienced by PMOs can be addressed in a study like this one. However, this subset will help to understand, at least partially, the context in which multiple PMOs exist and how this context makes them enter into mutual relationships or not. In all cases, IT acted as a driver in the formalization of project management. Formalization of project management was high almost everywhere except in health care where most PMOs at regional and local levels were rather new to project management implementation. These later PMOs did neither consider project management as being a core expertise in the health care

Table 4-13. Synoptic View on Case Studies' Major Characteristics

Case Descriptive Element		Telecom	Healthcare	Bank	Pharma
Social World (Context)	Formalization of project management	High	Ministry level: High Elsewhere: Low	High	High
	Types of projects	IT projects for external clients	Clinical and administrative IT leadership: development at ministry level; implementation at regional and local levels	IT and other projects for internal clients	Mostly operations improvement
	Project manager's status	Professionally certified	Mostly consultants	No formal project management education	Internally certified
Governance (Project governance)	Stakeholders versus shareholders orientation	Both	Stakeholders	Stakeholders	Both
	Outcome focus versus compliance focus	HQ: compliance Lower level PMOs: outcome	Both: opposition between ministry level and regional and local levels	PMO managers: outcome PMO members: compliance	Strategic projects: outcome Tactical projects: compliance
Governance (Formal structure of PMOs)	Position within the hierarchy	At all levels	Most of them are within IT Some at the executive level	At all levels	Virtual PMO at top Functional PMOs
	Basic statement of PMOs mission	Being recognized as a world class PMO Provider and support of project management processes Management of projects	Implement project management culture Implement projects Support change management	Strong portfolio management Interface between business and IT	Project delivery
Governance (Governance of multiple PMOs)		Hierarchical structure: high differentiation, formalization ,and centralization	Hierarchical structure: high differentiation, low formalization and centralization (except for budget) Network structure in a shared governance	Network structure: shared governance, medium lead organization and low administrative organization	Hierarchical structure: medium differentiation, high formalization and centralization
Relationships (Roles)	Intensity in the three roles: controlling-serving-partnering	At top level: controlling Lower level: serving Regional level: partnering	Most of them are controlling Some, serving Very few partnering	At top level: controlling Local: serving Strategic role: partnering	Controlling
Relationships (Practices)	Learning mechanisms	More explicit knowledge at the higher level; more implicit at local level	More explicit knowledge at the higher level; more implicit at local level	Explicit	Explicit

business, nor a required skill for its personnel. Most projects were managed by consultants. Conversely, project management was part of the core business for Telecom and Pharma: they strongly encourage development of project management skills. Telecom was managing projects for external clients. This may have had an influence for this organization to prove their engagement towards recognized standards, a context factor that is different in the other case studies.

4.5.2 Governance

Project management governance. In all case studies, the multiple PMOs were aligned with the organizational hierarchy. Clearly, the overall project governance in the presence of multiple PMOs showed tensions. On stakeholders versus shareholders orientation, Telecom and Pharma do have PMOs at the higher level that were oriented towards shareholders while others had stakeholders' orientation. This situation may lead to difficulty in establishing priorities in projects as well as in assessing their performance. Top level PMOs would value financial return to shareholders, while other PMOs would value satisfaction of stakeholders (clients, project team members, etc.). The Health Care and Bank organizations adopted a stakeholders' orientation. This was in line with their organizational status, the former being in public sector and the later a cooperative bank.

Similar tensions exist when considering outcomes versus compliance focus, where high level PMOs would more likely push for compliance to project management standards rather than for outcomes. Conversely, lower-level PMOs focus on outcomes. This is a surprising statement. It would have been expected that strategic PMOs normally at higher level, would influence strategic outcomes while PMOs at tactical and operational levels would focus on processes and standards as suggested by, among others, J. K. Crawford (2010). For PMOs at the lower level this can be explained by the proximity they have through managing projects for their company while, simultaneously, facing the customer.

Governance of multiple PMOs. Governance of multiple PMOs emerged in two structures: hierarchical and network structure. Related analyses are shown in Table 4-14, which shows the multi-PMO governance approaches of the four cases. The two organizations operating in hypercompetitive markets (Telecom and Pharma) use hierarchical structures, whereas the organization operating in a stable market (Bank) uses a network structure and the public

Table 4-14. PMOs' Governance in Their Context

Hierarchical Structure (Mechanistic)			Network Structure (Organic)	
Hyper-Competitive Market		Stable (Public)	Stable (Public)	Stable (Mutual)
TELECOM	PHARMA	HEALTHCARE	HEALTHCARE	BANK
High differentiation	Medium differentiation	High differentiation	High shared governance	High shared governance
High formalization	High formalization	Low formalization	Low lead organization	Medium lead organization
High centralization	High centralization	High/low centralization	Low administrative organization	Low administrative organization

health care in a stable *market* makes use of both. This is contrary to existing theories, which suggest organic structures for hypercompetitive markets and hierarchical structures for stable markets (Burns & Stalker, 1994; Hedlund, 1994). These theories were developed to get away from the pure traditional hierarchical structure and to favor innovation. Since then, innovative forms of organizing have emerged such as, among others, matrix-organization, project-based organization (Larson, 2004). However, Pettigrew and Massini (2003) showed that these innovative forms appear less frequent than thought. However, interestingly, they also showed that hierarchy did not disappear when implementing new forms of organizing. New forms are added to traditional hierarchies. From the cross-analysis, it can be observed that PMO networks are more likely to be part of the hierarchical structure of the organization, even if projects may be implemented in a more organic type of structure. This is independent of the market, be it competitive or not.

To that end, the PMO network complements the functional organization's organization structure, whereby the simultaneous presence of organic and mechanistic structures through the PMO and the line organization provide the ground for project managers to go back and forth between these structures to solve their issues at hand. To that end, the PMO networks provide either stability in dynamic organizations or flexibility in mechanic organizations. The combination of both provides for the "medium level of structure" (that we had in many of our case studies), which Turner and Müller (2004) identified as being correlated with the most successful projects. That is, the balance between mechanistic and organic structure, which allows the project manager to autonomously solve day-to-day issues within the project, and forces the project manager to follow the project management methodology and formal organizational structures to the extent needed for the governance institutions to be comfortable with the project and its progress.

4.5.3 Structure of Relationships Between PMOs: Isolated Island, Network, or Community

This part of the cross-cases synthesis is central to studying the community of PMOs. Table 4-13 shows that all PMOs in the organization take part in a PMO network, but as will be shown, communities of PMOs were rather rare. Analysis of the relationships between PMOs shows strong similarities between the four cases. First, the controlling role was by far the most popular PMO role. All case studies did have controlling PMOs at their top level, and then, other PMOs adopted the serving or partnering roles. This result is not surprising; it rather confirms results from previous research. Aubry and Hobbs (2010) found that project monitoring and control was the PMO's most important function. This is in line with observations from Maylor, Brady, Cooke-Davies, and Hodgson (2006) who said that project management practices were going back to rationalization approaches as was suggested by the metaphor of the iron cage (DiMaggio & Powell, 1983). The distribution of PMOs roles will be analyzed in more detail in Chapter 5.

Results from the intercase analyses showed very little about the existence of *true* communities of PMOs. Learning mechanisms existed in all PMO networks. However, almost all knowledge is shared through explicit artifacts. Globally, there are very few places where the community could construct itself through developing shared values and offering opportunities to share, or take initiatives in sharing of knowledge and values. It seems like thick boundaries exist around PMOs. They are isolated islands. Practices are rather linked with explicit knowledge on knowing *what* instead of more dynamic learning on knowing *how*, as suggested through community of practice theory (see section 2.2.3).

4.6 Key Findings

This section summarizes the key findings from the description and analysis of the four case studies considered in this research and from the cross-cases synthesis.

- Multiple PMOs appeared to be rather complex phenomena within their organizations. They are complex in terms of the multiplicity of components and actors spread over all layers and the multitude of channels for their interaction.
- There seems to be an alignment between context, governance, and structure of relationships. For example, at Telecom, formalization was very high, governance structure of their multiple PMOs was hierarchical, and their relationship strongly oriented towards a controlling role.
- Governance of projects was a source of tensions. Orientation and focus are often in opposition from the top level PMO and the PMOs at the lower level. Surprisingly, PMOs at the top level focus on compliance to standards, while PMOs at the lower level focus on outcome. This result contradicts the general assumption that PMOs at top level are business and strategy oriented, while PMOs at the lower level are methodology and tactically oriented.
- Networks of PMOs were rather strong in their controlling role. This finding confirms previous studies' results and reincarnates the old question of rationalization of project management through high-levels of control, an approach which at first sight is at odds with the more organic approaches for innovation and projects. At second sight, however, it bears the merit of higher transparency of what is done in projects, as well as better management toward higher project management maturity and faster adaptation to changing market conditions through centralized management. All of these aspects are subjects of current movements toward better governmentality of projects. Thus, the approaches are in line with current movements in project governance.
- Mechanistic PMOs' networks are found in case companies in hyper-competitive markets, whereas organic PMO networks are found in stable markets. Again, at first sight this result contradicts the understanding of organizational design for innovation. A second thought reveals a possible need for a balance in organizational design, a kind of "Yin and Yang" where the mechanistic networks are needed as stable reference points in extremely dynamic contexts/markets, to standardize practices and to focus on the project at hand without being distracted by a constantly changing context. In the same way, it can be argued that organic PMO networks are needed in stable contexts in order to further develop the project management practice and mature project delivery capabilities.
- True communities of PMOs are rather rare. There were not that many resources invested in community development. Learning mechanisms existed but were strongly of explicit type with a focus on knowing *what* and neglected the knowing *how*.

Chapter 5

PMO Roles in PMO Networks

In Chapter 4, four case studies were described and analyzed and cross-cases were synthesized. This chapter aims at presenting the results from an in-depth qualitative cross-cases synthesis from the perspective of PMO roles in PMO networks and the impact these roles could have on organizations aiming for learning and innovation.

Results are presented in four sections. The first section introduces a typology of PMOs based on their relationships. A visual representation of their roles is proposed using a ternary diagram. The second section illustrates the result of the PMOs 'roles analyses. The third section addresses innovation through the concept of slack resources. The fourth and final section identifies the partnering role as a precondition for the formation of communities of PMOs.

5.1 A Typology of PMOs Based Upon Roles and Relationships

The conceptual framework (see Figure 2-2) includes components that capture relationships between PMOs based upon three base roles: controlling, serving, and partnering. The four case studies described in Chapter Four were analyzed using these roles. Conclusions from the case studies description showed that: (1) a single PMO takes various roles simultaneously at different degrees of intensity with different stakeholders; and (2) PMO networks, within a single organization, exhibit complex varieties of PMO role mixtures. This typological approach is best visualized by use of a ternary diagram.

A ternary diagram is a triangle, which displays the relative proportions of three possible categories of individual elements that make up an aggregate population. These categories must be mutually exclusive and collectively exhaustive (Plewe & Bagchi-Sen, 2001). A labor market, for instance, is composed of employment, which is either primary (agriculture), secondary (manufacturing), or tertiary (services) (Preusser, 1976). Ternary diagrams are a graphical technique, which is common in various disciplines such as demography, geography, chemistry, or pedology. They are used to represent tri-variate data in which the three variables represent proportions of a whole (Graham & Midgley, 2000), such as the composition of a territorially bounded population by age (adolescent, adult, retired) or ethnicity (Plewe & Bagchi-Sen, 2001) or the composition of a population of school children by public, private, or postsecondary schools (Patterson, Urban, Myers, Bhaduri, Bright, & Coleman, 2007). In the context of PMOs, serving, controlling and partnering are clearly exclusive role elements that combine into an aggregate role profile. Within a three-dimensional role space, each theoretical mix of roles can be plotted as a specific role profile.

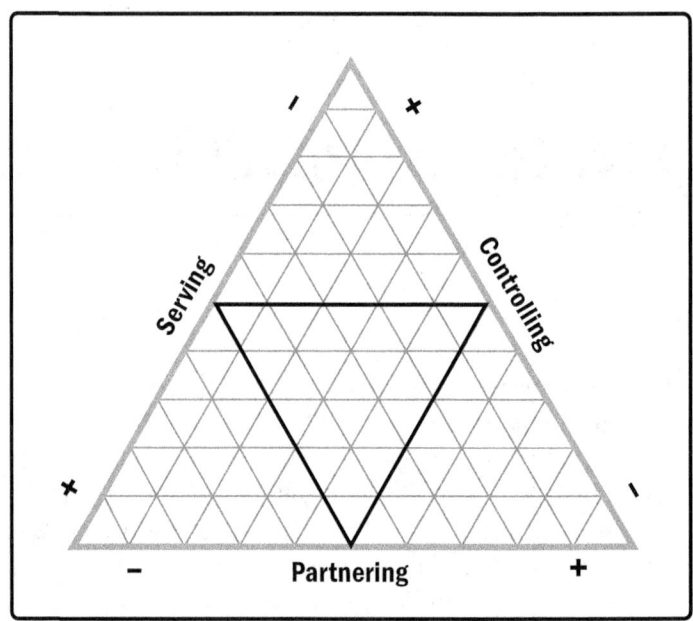

Figure 5-1. The PMO Role Triangle

For reasons of simplicity, we distinguish four role regions based upon role profiles (see Figure 5-1): the controlling role profile (top), the serving role profile (left), the partnering role profile (right), and a balanced profile in the center without a focused orientation. Every PMO role profile can now be located in this role space. Within this conceptual framework of a ternary role space, any concrete combination of roles that a PMO exerts can be associated with a particular role region and thus be located as a ternary role profile. The diagram can be used for different scales of analysis, that is, at the level of the PMO (mapping the distinct activities), at the level of the organization (mapping the different PMOs), or at the level of a group of organizations (mapping the distinct PMO cultures for a set of organizations).

5.2 PMOs' Roles

The case studies' role analyses presented in Chapter Four can therefore be pursued using the role triangle. In this section, a cross-case synthesis is presented comprising the four case studies. As illustrated in Figure 5-2, PMO networks can be drawn for each of the case studies showing interesting results about PMO relationships.

5.2.1 PMOs in Controlling Roles

Except with Pharma, PMOs show a variety of role profiles. PMOs at the upper apex in the control profile are positioned higher in the organizational hierarchy than other PMOs. They are accountable for aggregated project results in terms of scope, budget, and time. It is obvious in Telecom and Bank, where PMOs at the top level have direct formal authority over PMOs at the regional level. In the Health Care case study, the two control profile PMOs are not in a position of formal authority over the other PMOs but they established relationships

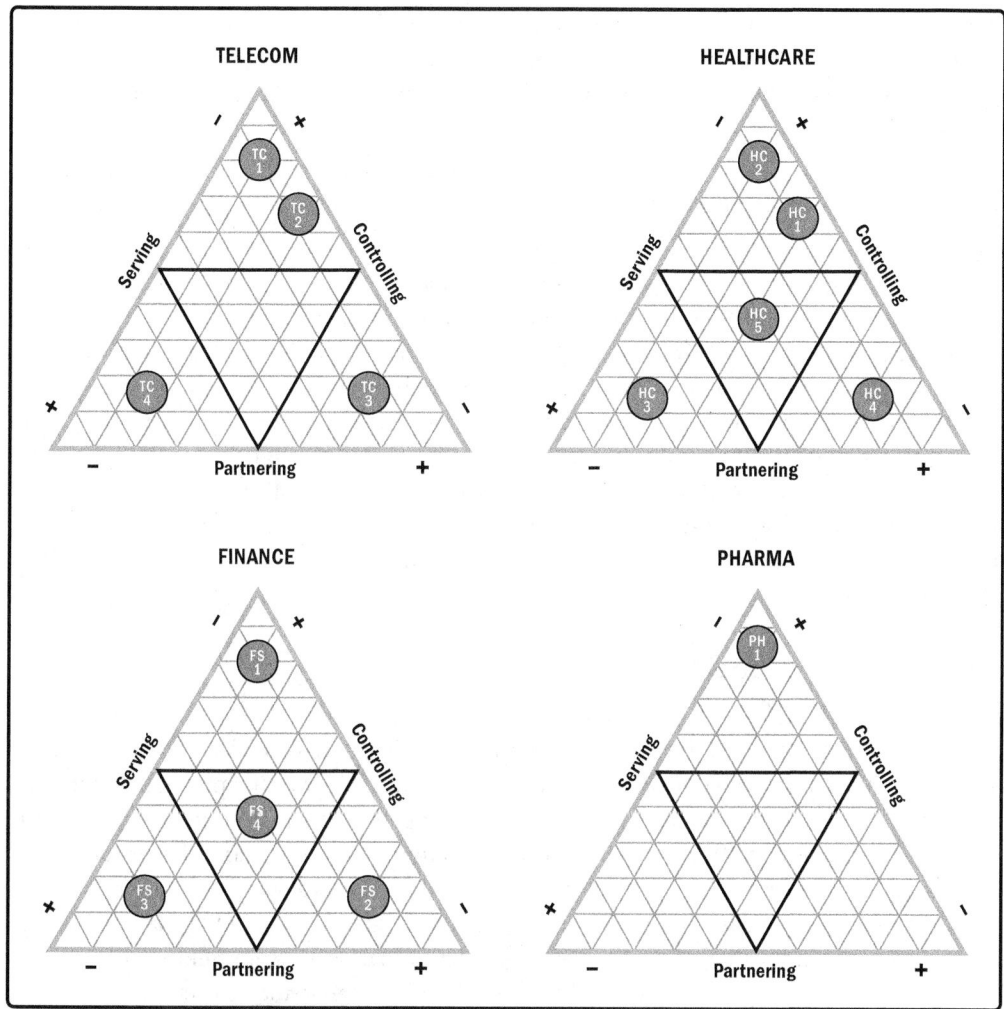

Figure 5-2. The Four Case Study Triangles

through projects and by sharing of the authority for controlling them. In Pharma, the virtual PMO has authority over project managers, for example, by doing the annual performance evaluation of project managers.

Altogether, the position of PMOs within the triangle and the analysis of their position within the organizational chart may be contrasted with the hierarchical PMO model suggested by J. K. Crawford (2010) where multiple PMOs coexist at different hierarchical levels without obvious relationships.

5.2.2 PMOs in Serving Roles

PMOs in serving roles are contracted or otherwise engaged to perform work for others. In three of the four cases, PMOs were directly managing projects. The servicing role can include, for example, the provision of project management services from a regional PMO to a country level PMO by managing a project on behalf of the country level PMO. This happened occasionally in the Telecom case, where the regional PMO provided project managers in case a country organization were lacking skills or resources to manage projects themselves.

5.2.3 PMOs in Partnering Roles

The partnering apex shows a diversified picture in terms of PMO roles. In Telecom, the regional level PMO supports and helps in troubled projects. This function is likely to succeed in a partnership type of relationship, where organizational learning is valued instead of a blame culture, where the search for the "guilty" prevails. In Health Care, the serving PMO maintains a rich network of opportunities through involvement of its director at different organizational levels. Through this leadership, many new project management initiatives were identified and implemented on a voluntary basis and diffused throughout the PMO network. In Bank, the co-equal PMO, in its partnering role, is chartered with a strategic mandate to translate between business and IT. In this particular case, partnership appears to open up the dialogue between stakeholders who often have different perspectives on projects and their outcomes.

5.2.4 PMOs in a Central Role

In the center of the triangle are the PMOs with a balanced role. They are at equilibrium in terms of intensity of controlling, serving, and partnering roles. Two PMOs are at this position. In Health Care, the balanced PMO has a controlling role over the projects it manages, because of pressure from upper levels to respect budgets and make projects contribute to return-on-investment (ROI). This has to be done in the context of a rather low level of project management standardization. The approach this PMO developed with other PMOs in clinical projects is to serve and to help project participants to grow and learn using a constructive approach. Furthermore, this PMO also developed partnership relations with other functional units, which otherwise would have possibly entered into power struggles with them (Aubry et al., 2011). In short, the balanced PMO at Health Care undertook deliberate actions in all three roles to manage project results. In the Bank PMO, the risk of tension was rather low due to the non-existence of hierarchical relations (and their power struggles). The intensity of this PMO in balancing roles was only at a moderate level.

5.3 Slack and Innovativeness Through Partnering Roles

In this section, a cross-case synthesis is presented taking an integrative view of the 27 PMOs investigated in this research. Figure 5-3 is used as a starting point to suggest a new interpretation of the qualitative case studies.

Figure 5-3 shows that the PMO role distribution in the PMO role triangle tends towards controlling and serving roles, rather than partnering roles. This is indicated by the diagonal line. However, some of the circles stand for more than one individual PMO. By taking into account the number of individual PMOs, results show that there are 10 in controlling roles and five in serving roles, out of 21 PMOs. Therefore, 71 percent of PMOs perform controlling and serving roles. Five PMOs (29 percent) perform partnering roles.

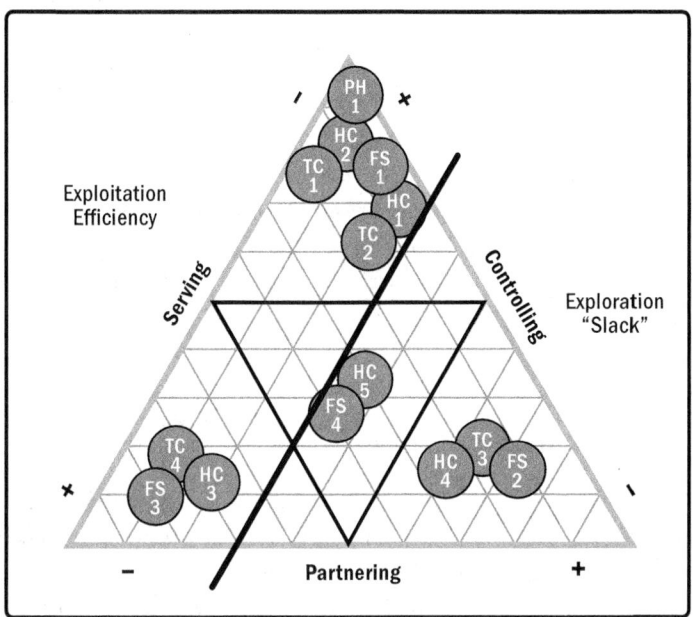

Figure 5-3. Integrative View on PMO Roles

Controlling is the most common role and is associated with the PMO function of monitoring and controlling projects or other PMOs. This result is in line with previous studies, which showed that this function is the most important PMO function, and one that is under the mandate of most PMOs (Hobbs & Aubry, 2010). Conversely, the serving role is associated with a rather collaborative approach in respect to internal clients. In this role, a PMO is more likely to offer services to project management stakeholders.

The serving PMO negotiates its own mandate to respond to the specific needs of stakeholders and to respect the relationship with them (Huemann, 2010). Instead of imposing a methodology, a process, or a tool, this approach implies that the PMO adapts its solution to the needs and the degree of formalization of the stakeholder or institution it serves. These PMOs are at a risk of being rejected with their offers. Being rejected may threaten the PMOs' legitimacy, as shown by Hobbs and Aubry (2010), who identified that 50 percent of all PMOs were put into question within the last two years of their existence. Avoiding conflict to maintain PMO survival was the strategy of some of the PMOs in the serving role.

Developing partnerships with stakeholders takes time and requires long-term relationships. It may seem curious to invest resources in long term partnership knowing that projects are temporary organizations (Lundin & Söderholm, 1995) and that PMOs are transitioning over time as does the context and the organization (Aubry et al., 2011). This is the point where the role of the PMO emerges as a leader in knowledge sharing between different project management stakeholders. An example from the Health Care case is the dialogue that has opened up on process development between a PMO and the HR department. The PMO has the mandate of reviewing almost all clinical processes within the new hospital construction project. Process development was part of the HR department that first reacted against the PMO. However, the PMO director managed to involve the HR department in jointly reviewing how this work should be undertaken in the specific context of this large project. They both agreed that the HR department should embark on the journey together with the PMO. For the PMO director, this was the only way to succeed in the long term.

This partnering role is not an ad hoc way of working. It is based on foundations, such as values and shared vision, which are pervasive to all their relationships.

A common characteristic from PMOs in partnership roles is that they are part of the governance of their network. They do not feel at risk, or if they feel it, they act to pursue their vision and to influence decision makers. They are risk takers.

5.4 Key Findings

This section sums up the key findings from the role analysis of the PMOs in the four case studies.

- Ternary diagrams are appropriate tools to display the role variety of PMOs in multi-PMO settings. Ternary diagrams are applicable at different levels, for example to visualize distinct roles within individual PMOs, to show the roles of individual PMOs in multi-PMO settings, or to visualize different PMO cultures across groups of organizations. The present research showed the role distribution of individual PMOs in PMO hierarchies and PMO networks.
- The application of the ternary network showed that all organizations assign a controlling role to their PMOs. Second in popularity is the serving role, which is followed by the partnering role. The balanced role is least often found. A timely order in development may be indicated by this. That means, initially a controlling role is assigned to a new PMO; once that is established, the serving and then the partnering roles develop. Finally, the balanced role is established. This is, of course, subject to many contingencies, such as structure of the multi-PMO setting, their charters, market dynamics, and value of project management, to name but a few.
- The interpretation of the ternary diagram from the perspective of knowledge management showed that the two most popular roles of PMOs relate to exploitation of existing knowledge, whereas the less popular roles relate to exploration of new knowledge. Assuming the timely development indicated earlier, this implies that only the more developed PMO networks actively explore new knowledge for future innovation or improved competitiveness. Given the importance of new knowledge for innovation and long-term survival in the marketplace, this clearly indicates an area for improvement in PMO charters. A more balanced distribution of PMO roles at the outset may therefore be indicated.
- Partnering was identified as the role that best allows for knowledge exchange. Fostering a partnering role in PMO networks allows for creating resource slack, which is often referred to as a condition for innovation. Resource slack provides for the time and resources needed to actively explore new knowledge and develop new insights, which subsequently lead to innovation and long-term prosperity.
- The partnering role is more likely to share knowledge within a multi-PMO setting. Therefore, it constitutes a precondition for the formation of an effective Community of Practice. Another indicator for the importance of a partnering role within multi-PMO settings.

Chapter 6

PMO Network and Knowledge Exchange in the Pharma Case Study

The main goal of this chapter is to develop of the concept of multiple PMOs towards the concept of networked PMOs. Earlier chapters and the qualitative case studies in particular (see Chapter Four), have shown that PMOs, and accordingly people in PMOs, sustain diverse relationships of monitoring, control, assistance, advise, and exchange between each other. While until now the analysis has focused on the qualitative aspects of these interactions, this chapter presents a quantitative network analysis by focusing on the structure of PMO network interactions. The goal is to empirically explore the notion of networks of PMOs: based on one extensive network case study, the Pharma case, which investigates how PMOs contribute to interpersonal networks of knowledge exchange in the corporate project management community.

This chapter presents results from the quantitative research using visual and analytical methods of social network analysis (SNA). The study is based on a quantitative, web-based questionnaire targeted at all 90 project managers in the Pharma organization. The project managers came from different managerial ranks and were in this role in 2008 and/or 2009. Nine project managers had already left the company or were on maternity leave by the time of the survey. Eighty-nine responses were achieved, which equals a response rate of 99 percent (see section 3.3). All employees worked in the same firm geographical location, but their workplaces were distributed across various buildings on that site.

6.1 Project Managers Approve PMO Performance

It is striking how much satisfaction project managers reported with respect to the performance of their PMO (see Table 6-1). The descriptive analysis of responses shows that employees reject the notion that they can produce equivalent results without the PMO or their fellow project managers. Moreover, they reported that the PMO had proved effective over the past years. Support was mostly received in the areas of monitoring and supervising of projects, as well as provision of project management tools and methods. Project managers said they were eager to help each other and depended on each other's advice. However, most employees did only partially agree with the statement that their knowledge was being

Table 6.1: Importance of PMO and Knowledge Sharing

Statements to be Evaluated by the Respondents	Disagree					Agree
My projects would have produced the same results without the PMO.	46	22	13	5	3	0
I do not need any help from the PMO in this firm.	68	13	7	0	1	0
I do not need any help from fellow project managers.	71	8	9	1	0	0
The PMO support has been effective for my projects over the last years.	0	4	16	28	41	0
I have benefited from the PMO in this firm.	1	3	12	22	51	0
My fellow project managers turn to me frequently to seek my advice.	5	11	52	15	6	0
My fellow project managers have adopted and used parts of my project management know-how to improve their project management practice.	7	10	33	17	20	0
I am eager to help my fellow project manager whenever they need advice.	0	0	3	8	78	0
I would like to see more knowledge exchange and contact with other project managers in this firm.	1	1	4	14	69	0
Exchanging more knowledge between project managers would increase the performance of the company.	1	1	6	18	63	0

N = 89 project managers belonging to the PMO

asked for or used by their fellow project managers. Generally, there was a strong belief that a more intensive exchange of knowledge and higher levels of knowledge-based communication would leverage the performance of the company.

This result is in line with previous research from Hobbs and Aubry (2011) on 500 PMOs showing that the recognition of PMO's expertise is one of the four variables explaining the performance of project and programs. However, the same research showed that respondents ranked competency improvement of PMO personal as the second most important element (Hobbs & Aubry, 2010).

6.2 Project Managers Overestimate Their Role as Knowledge Providers

The social network analysis reveals the patterns of dyadic interaction between project managers in the corporation. Therefore, the relationships of an actor (i.e., a member of the project management community) are most important. Two questions were asked to identify dyadic relationships: first, who are the people I help? Second, who are the people who help me (see section 3.3)? The results for question 1 are shown in Figure 6-1. It shows the majority of knowledge provision happened within the survey group (i.e., between the black nodes). The 89 responding employees named another 115 contacts (grey nodes) inside or outside the firm to exchange knowledge. The analysis focuses on the 89 project managers at the core of Figure 6-1.

Theoretically, the two questions are redundant because if help is sent from an actor it should consequently arrive at the help seeker. Accordingly, if senders respond to question 1, recipients should confirm the same linkage in question 2. In a world of perfect conscience, the two networks generated from these questions should be identical.

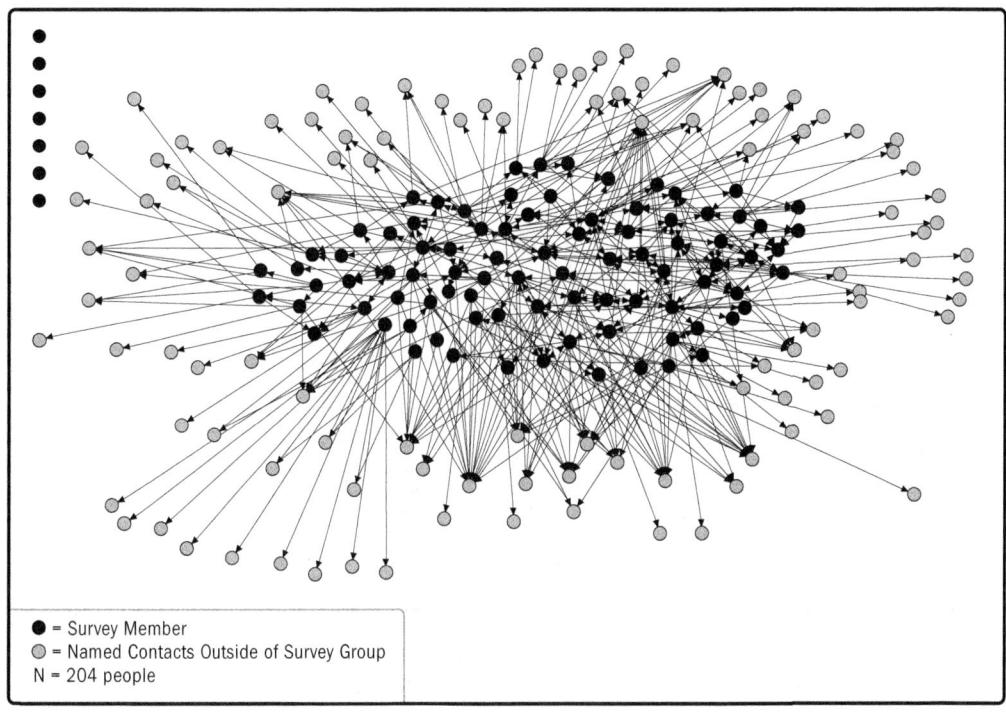

Figure 6-1. Providers of Project Management Knowledge

However, in reality they are not (see Figure 6-2). Figure 6-2a shows the initial exchange that employees reported, while Figure 6-2b shows the exchanges to have been confirmed their colleagues. While Figure 6.2a shows 196 relationships between employees, the number reduces to less than half (87 relations) in Figure 6.2b. In Figure 6.2a there are only 6 employees who were not provided with help according to the information provided by the other colleagues, whereas there are already 29 employees who have not provided any help in Figure 6.2b. This comparison suggests at least two interpretations: (1) employees tend to overestimate their importance in knowledge provision; and (2) recipients do not always acknowledge or value the appropriation of new knowledge or that they do not credit new knowledge to the source of that transfer. For reasons of robustness, the following analyses are based on the more conservative measure of "who are the people that helped me," and it therefore studies only those relations through which knowledge was actually received and credited by a source (Figure 6-2b).

6.3 PMO Members Gain Little Prestige in Interpersonal Knowledge Flow

The visual assessment of the knowledge transfer network within the PMO suggests that knowledge transfer related to project management is well developed between individual project managers (see Figure 6-3). There seems to be a rich structure of peer-to-peer knowledge transfer. On average, members of the PMO and expert group (as described

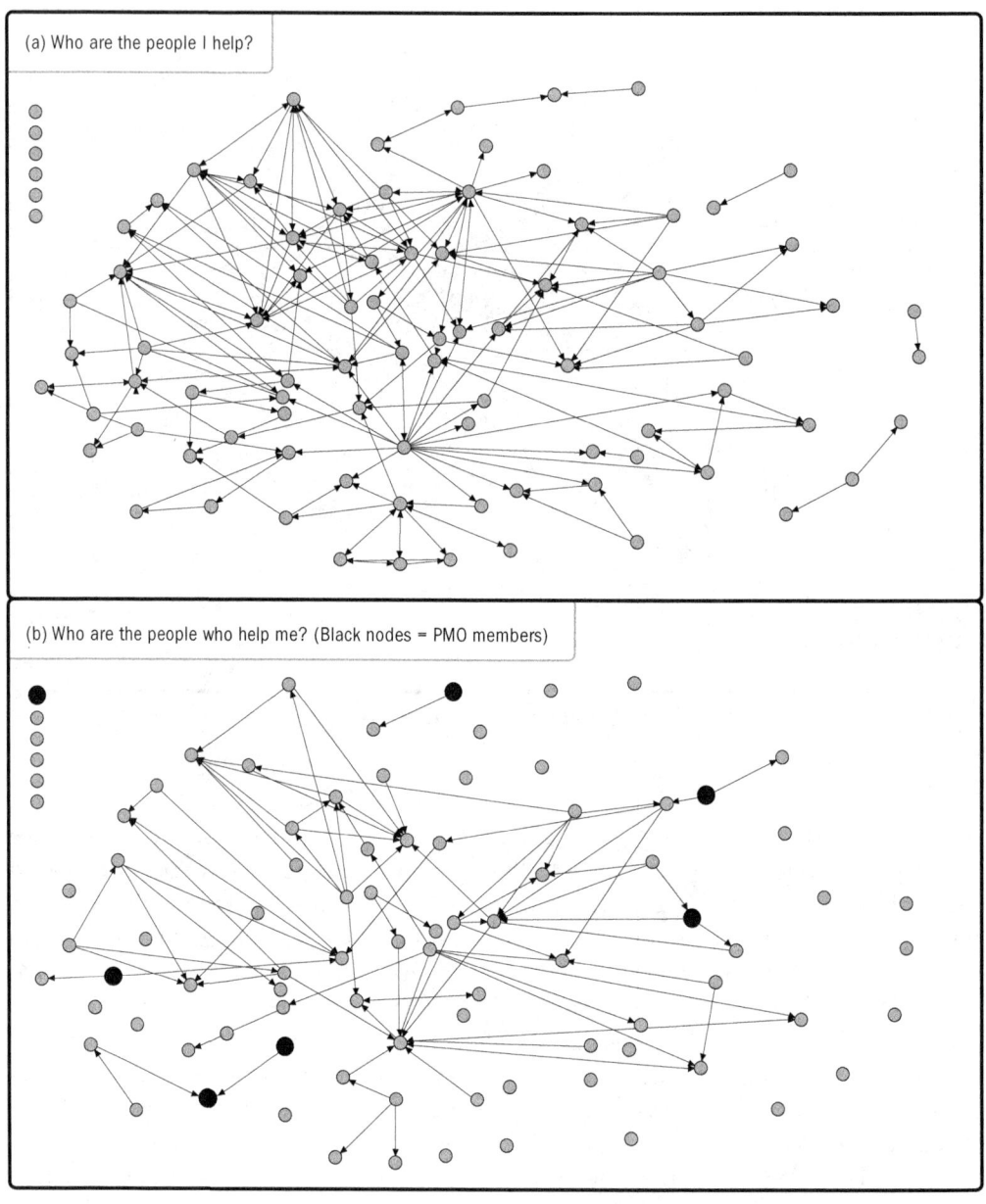

Figure 6-2. The Problem of Measuring Interpersonal Knowledge Transfer

in section 4.4.3) provide help slightly more often than project managers do. However, PMO members seem to be less central than many project managers in the overall knowledge network. A more robust assessment of the relational prestige that a manager obtains in a network is the measure of outdegree. Outdegree equals the number of contacts that an actor has provided with knowledge and who have credited that knowledge receipt to him or her as a source. The higher the outdegree of an employee, the greater is his or

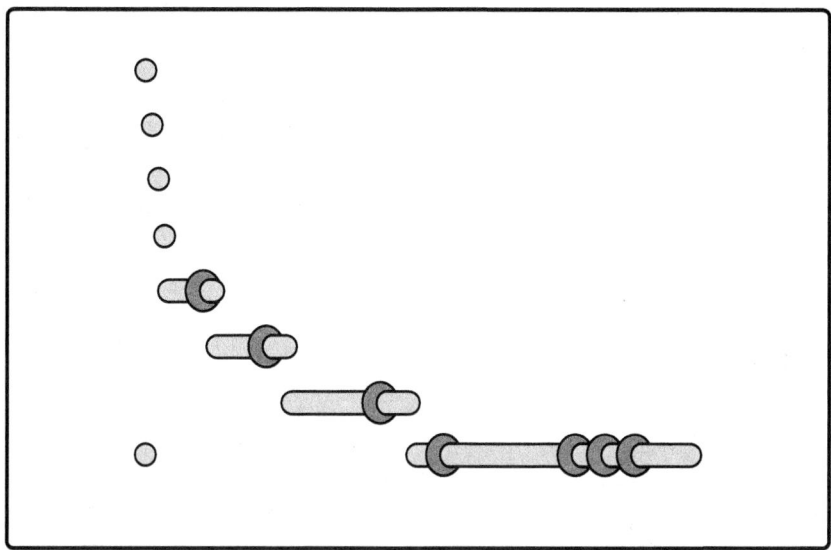

Figure 6.3. Rank Order of Project Managers Who are Credited for Knowledge Provision to Other Project Managers

her prestige in the knowledge network. The distribution of the prestige of the individual managers is shown in Figure 6-3. The top group of knowledge providers is composed of all regular project managers that have been credited as source of new knowledge by up to seven other colleagues. In contrast, none of the members of the PMO and expert group achieves any comparable level of prestige. Instead, they seem to be less prominent in the knowledge provision network and do not differ significantly from regular project managers. In fact, 20 project managers (nearly a quarter of the sample) achieve higher prestige than the average PMO and expert group member.

6.4 Quasi-Islands of Knowledge Exchange

The knowledge network shows the pattern of knowledge flows through the organization. The flow of interpersonal knowledge is fragmented into four distinct clusters of employees and one residual group of so-called isolates. These are individuals who don't share knowledge with any of the other project managers. From the 97 relationships, 90 percent are captured within the clusters and only 10 relationships stretched across these cluster boundaries (see Figure 6-4). Three clusters are made up of 12 people, one of 22. Furthermore, there is a residual group of 31 isolates. Each cluster has a member of the PMO team/ expert group in it. The clusters are relatively homogeneous in terms of the characteristics of its members: gender, age, the year starting in the current position, and the highest degree of education do not vary significantly. Clusters are also similar with respect to the share of people who have suggested new best practices and who have seen these practices being used. The only significant difference between the clusters is the average work experience. In the big cluster, 22 employees had the strongest experience with a mean number

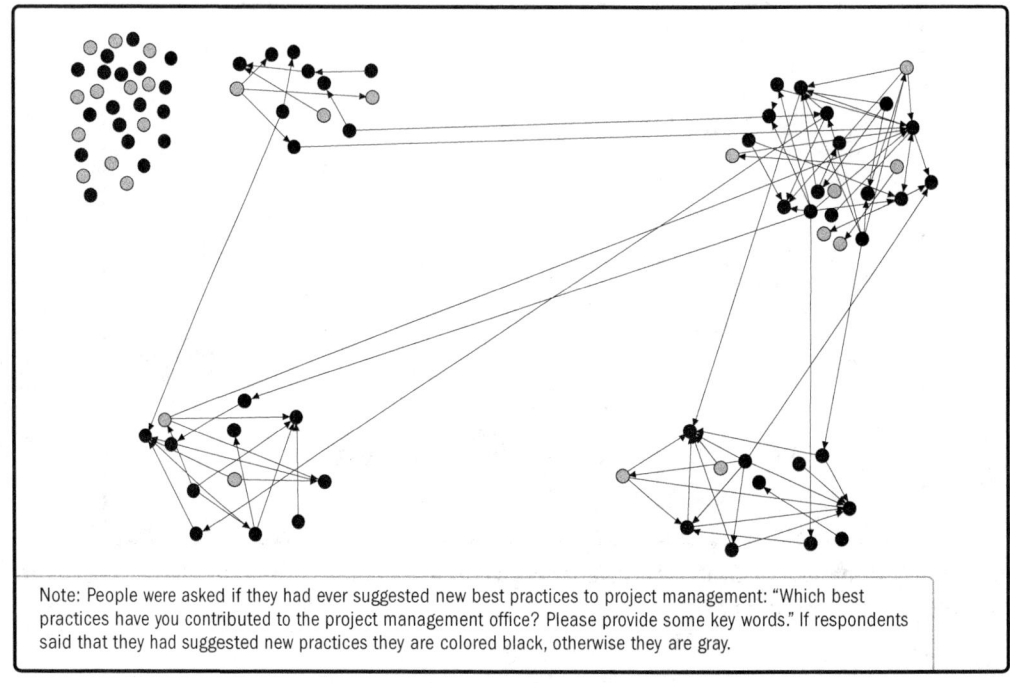

Note: People were asked if they had ever suggested new best practices to project management: "Which best practices have you contributed to the project management office? Please provide some key words." If respondents said that they had suggested new practices they are colored black, otherwise they are gray.

Figure 6-4. Four Clusters of Knowledge Sharing

of completed projects of 17.14. The isolates were the group with the least amount of projects worked on (mean = 7.10). The other three clusters (each made up of 12 employees) varied between mean numbers of 8.08, 10.58, and 15.83 projects.

Who are these boundary spanners? Apparently, those individuals who maintain relationships between clusters are always people who have contributed new best practices to the PMO. This observation suggest that spanning an own group of redundant communication requires some energy and initiative taking for managers. Only a subset of those who also contributed to new knowledge creation did that.

6.5 Future Knowledge-Sharing Comes With Prior Collaboration

Does previous collaboration in project teams enhance future knowledge exchange? To challenge this expectation, the network of knowledge sharing is compared with the historically cumulated pattern of prior project collaboration between all employees. Figure 6-5 displays (a) the network of interpersonal knowledge exchange and (b) a co-membership network showing who worked together with whom on projects in 2008 and 2009. The analysis of the overlap of the relations demonstrates that nearly two thirds of all knowledge sharing relations (62.1 percent of "who provided me with PM-knowledge") were also found in the co-membership network of prior project collaboration. These results indicate that prior collaboration in joint projects provides the opportunity for establishing trust and identifying

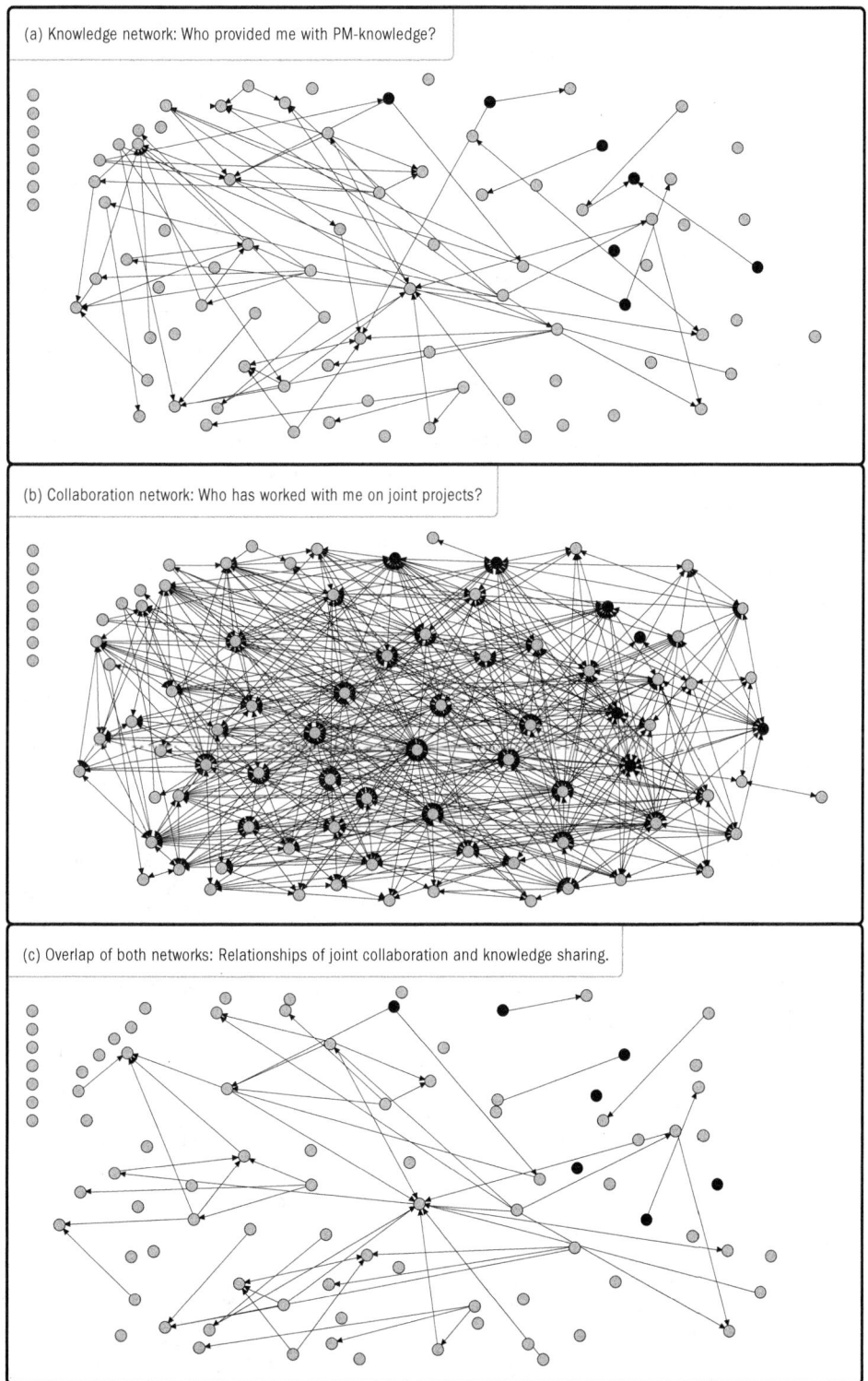

Figure 6-5. Prior Project Collaboration Eases Subsequent Knowledge Circulation

others' expertise to draw from in the future. Collaboration, therefore, increases the likelihood to share knowledge in the future.

6.6 Key Findings

1. People tend to overestimate their importance as knowledge providers. Less than 50 percent of the relations reported as being "sent" were acknowledged as being "received." Therefore, the analysis focused on the acknowledged reception of knowledge. Project managers in the Pharma case study actively shared project management knowledge with their colleagues, and they valued this knowledge transfer.
2. Although project managers widely appreciated the role of the PMO, the network analysis found that the PMO did not occupy a pronounced role in dyadic knowledge transfer. PMO members (including the expert group) only reached average centrality in distributing knowledge across the network. Moreover, PMO members seemed not to share any project management knowledge with each other. They transferred knowledge exclusively to project managers but were isolated among each other.
3. Ninety percent of all interpersonal knowledge transfer relations were captured by four distinct clusters of project managers, each focusing on one PMO member. Only the most innovative employees exchanged knowledge across these clusters.
4. Time constraints were reported to be the prime barrier to more effective knowledge transfer. Almost half of all employees found their daily workload to be critical barriers for an intensified knowledge transfer. In contrast, a quarter of all respondents didn't detect any barrier at all. Therefore, most project managers wanted to intensify knowledge exchange, and they were convinced that this would leverage corporate performance.
5. Some managers suggested to increase the involvement of people from other functional departments in projects and case studies (e.g., to analyze the advantages and disadvantages from one case). This suggestion reflects the high fragmentation of know-how between the PMO managers and their virtual communities of project managers that was identified in the network analysis. More trainings, meetings, and overall interpersonal exchange were desired and the creation of meeting places was an important concern in the survey.

Chapter 7

Discussion

Some of the key findings from this research merit more attention to better understand the phenomenon of PMO networks and their contribution to the knowledge sharing and innovation.

7.1 Communities of PMOs: Diagnostic and Opportunities

Existence of communities of practices and more specifically communities of PMOs may carry a desirability bias. Organizations in general would appreciate being associated with such communities. Findings show that PMOs are often linked together in networks in their serving, controlling, and partnering roles. While they mainly serve the organization objectives, very few of them could be defined as a *true* community of PMOs for two major raisons. First, most of these PMO networks are structured within the organizational hierarchy in a top-down controlling way without any explicit ambition regarding knowledge creation and sharing. These results confirm the deep-rooted perception of project management as maintaining a Taylorism paradigm (Williams, 2005) or creating an iron cage (Maylor et al., 2006). This is also in line with findings in research on the most important PMO function, which are controlling and serving (Hobbs & Aubry, 2010). This is not to say that PMOs should not control projects, but by overemphasizing this particular role, the organization may forgive opportunities to leverage from knowledge dynamics in projects that foster innovation, which ultimately leads to winning over competition. In this case, it is not the distortion of the initial concept of community of practice (Duguid, 2008a), it is the inexistence of such a community.

Second, associated with the former is the lack of the sense of the community. There are two parts in the suggested definition of a community of PMOs: community and PMOs' practices (see Figure 2-3). Results presented focus on the latter. Learning mechanisms have been identified, much of them being of explicit nature, thereby giving a strong accent to the *what* and forgetting about the *how*. More importantly, PMO networks did not show sharing of values, willingness to share or initiative taking. There was not much boundary management, which was well defined and, at the same time, open to others. This was observed in the small number of PMOs performing a partnering role. Welcoming structures to initiate the newcomers were exceptional. Yet, PMO networks rarely are true communities of PMOs.

Adopting a positive look at these findings, there are opportunities for organizations in adopting a communities of PMOs approach. It is clear that it falls under the managerial paradox as claimed by Duguid (2008a) as being a managerial instrument instead of an emerging phenomenon from the workers. Authors acknowledge that communities of PMOs are instruments that contribute to the organizational performance through knowledge management and innovation. But project management managers (e.g., PMO manager, portfolio or program managers) are direct actors within these communities. Paraphrasing Schön (1983), they are reflective managers as exemplified in Blomquist and Müller (2006). These managers have to create an environment where not only explicit PMO practices could be discussed and then kept in databases, but also where practices and values could be shared openly and where a sense of a community might emerge. Such an environment will encourage implicit knowledge sharing and a true community of PMOs to exist. In doing so, managers provide the necessary slack associated with the innovation and with the partnering role.

7.2 Revisiting the Conceptual Framework for Communities of PMOs

The previous discussion leads to revisiting the initial conceptual framework (see Figure 2-3) to include the relation between the structure of the relationships between PMOs and their contribution to the organizational performance, as expressed in terms of slack, innovativeness, and ambidexterity (see Figure 7-1). This revised conceptual framework is based upon the assumption

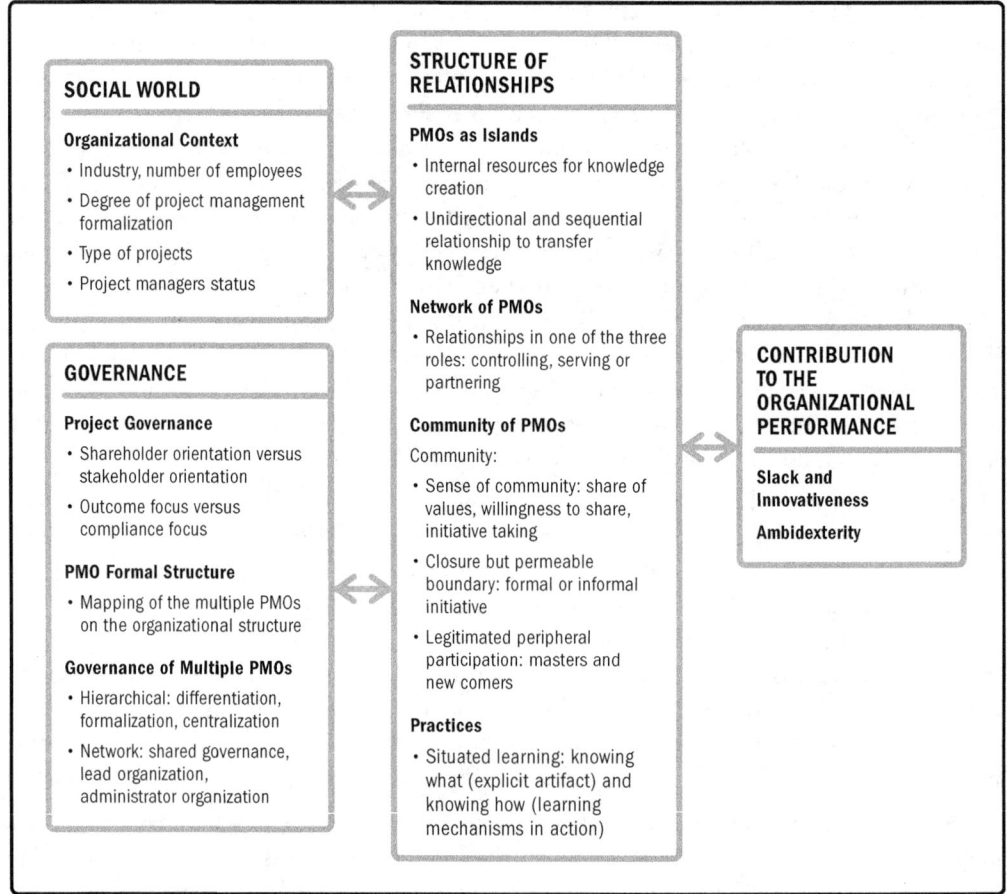

Figure 7-1. Revised Conceptual Framework for Communities of PMOs

that innovation is essential for organizations to grow and survive. Project management per se has a direct link with the management of innovation. Organizational learning is essential to innovate. It is argued that communities of PMOs are a good approach to organizational learning. To make this learning happen, slack is needed. In terms of communities of PMOs, slack refers to resources and time to develop partnering types of relationships. Findings show very few examples of slack. An example of slack was found in the Health Care case study, where a common change management process was developed jointly between the PMO and the HR department. In other words, partnering is a precondition for the formation of communities of PMOs.

Running for innovation or exploration is essential to succeed, but organizations must also maintain their exploitation capabilities. The latter capabilities are mostly obtained through controlling and serving roles. Ambidexterity refers to the ability of doing both.

This revised conceptual framework should not serve as a prescriptive formulation. It should rather serve as a reflection to guide assessments of particular situations of multiple PMOs. There is not one best way. As for single PMOs, there is a wide variety of configurations to make the overall system to contribute to the organizational performance. Social world is a basic parameter in the community of practice theory, and social world along with its governance form a unique environment.

7.3 The Bagel Metaphor Describing PMOs' Networks

There is a particular PMO network pattern that was drawn from case studies and that merits some further attention. In this pattern, the network of PMOs is has a central PMO at the top level and multiple other PMOs at various layers of the organizational hierarchy. As shown in our case studies, the higher level PMO adopts a controlling role over the other PMOs, while other PMOs at lower levels would rather show serving and partnering roles. From a community of PMOs perspective, the central PMO uses explicit knowledge sharing practices while the others had, to certain limits, a mix of types of knowledge sharing practices. Interestingly, these PMOs do not include the central high-level PMO within their relationships for knowledge creation and sharing. This situation resulted in an empty center in the middle of the PMO network that can be visualized through a doughnut or bagel metaphor (see Figure 7-2).

The central PMO is located in an "ivory tower," typically in a corporate headquarters. It focuses on corporate wide improvement of project results, that is, the aggregate results of all projects undertaken. Their related improvement activities are therefore of a general nature and may or may not help local PMOs in projects or at the country level. Given the managerial power and controlling role of the central PMO, the lower level PMOs are reluctant to involve the central PMO into their day-to-day problems or alert them in case project results get compromised. There are a number of reasons for this:

- The central PMO may provide input to the annual performance appraisal of the lower level PMO members. The PMO members do not want to make their faulty projects visible to those who evaluate their performance.
- The central PMO may start a series reviews and audits to identify the root cause for the project's deviation from plan, which means additional work and more "bureaucracy"

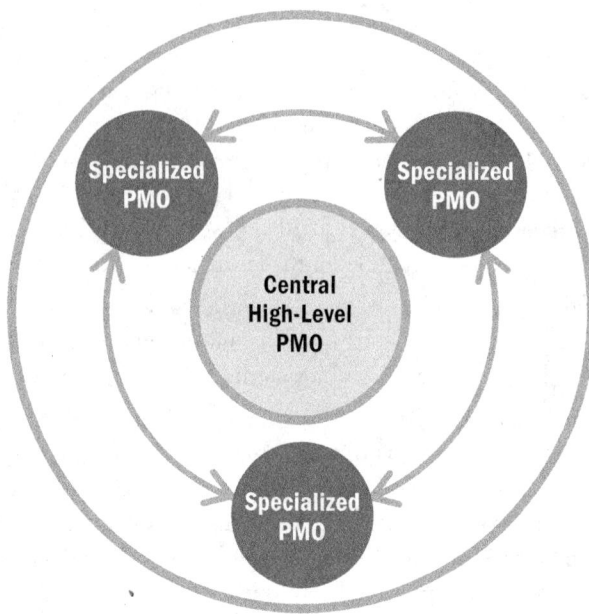

Figure 7.2. The Bagel Metaphor Describing Multi-PMOs Relationships

at the project level. That happens at a time when the resources are already strained for achieving the ever more unreachable project goals.

- Visibility of compromised project results often leads to more reporting and other communication, which again "comes on top" of the workload of an already strained workforce.
- Admitting to work on projects with compromised objectives may be perceived as a career-limiting event and therefore not communicated to institutions that have a say in the promotion of individuals.

Central PMOs are therefore at the risk of developing a different perspective towards the business than their "customer facing" lower level PMOs, thereby becoming excluded from reality at the project level. This is supported by the governance paradigms figures of Telecom, Health Care, and Bank (see Figures 4-1, 4-2, and 4-3), where lower level PMOs (or PMO members) were managed using significantly different governance approaches than the central Headquarters PMO. Central PMOs should therefore aim for partnering roles with their lower level PMOs in order to maintain information flows and provide value when possible.

Chapter 8

Conclusion

This monograph constitutes the research report on Governance and Communities of PMOs. It aimed at providing a better understanding of the phenomenon of the coexistence of multiple PMOs in large organizations. Constant quest for more and more efficiency gives persistent pressure to find out ways to not reinventing the wheel and to act from existing assets. Given the highly competitive economic world in which all organizations evolve, this research took the communities of practices perspective to explore the knowledge sharing between PMOs. This approach was fruitful in providing rich descriptions of four case studies in four economic sectors and three continents from which analysis provided promising avenues for the future.

This research was innovative in several aspects. First, the team brings together researchers from two academic fields: project management and geographical sociology. Both illuminate the phenomenon in a novel way. More specifically, looking at PMOs in a relationship perspective enlightens the strength and weaknesses of project management structure. Knowledge sharing is a key driver to innovation and innovation is essential for succeeding in the marketplace. Projects being temporary organizations, entities such as PMOs could play a more crucial role in knowledge creation and sharing. Our results show just the contrary. PMOs are more likely to be in a controlling and serving role and neglect to develop their partnering role. Following March (1991) with the ambidexterity concept, PMOs should play on the two sides of operations and exploration. But exploration is not free. Investments in slack resources are required. In terms of multiple PMOs, this can be translated in giving time to project team member or PMO member to simply share their values and unique experiences in nontraditional event, or to favor internal partnership. All this represents a cost in the short term, but it also may represent economy for future development. It can take the form of a community of PMOs, or other forms. The goal is to turn project management knowledge into action.

Second, it provides some evidence of a crucial lack of knowledge creation and sharing in PMO networks (within the limitation of the four case studies). Communities of PMOs are more likely to be desirable by the project management managers and professionals but they are not yet part of the reality.

Limitations from case studies methodology refrain from being prescriptive. However, these case studies provided some evidence of what should help managers as well as academics in their future development.

Implications for management:

1. Organizational design: managers involved in the overall organizational project management design will certainly gain some new insights for better design of multiple PMO settings and their spread over different levels of the organization, thereby taking into account the nature of PMO relationships. As our results show, a PMO's mandate emphasizing controlling or serving roles will contribute to the exploitation of well-known processes. On the contrary, a PMO's mandate emphasizing a partnering role contributes to exploration and innovation. Balancing these roles gives the flexibility to the organization to work both ways, which is ambidexterity.
2. The reflexive manager in project management: innovation is only possible with slack. Our results should help managers to find their own avenue to favor explicit and tacit knowledge to be created and shared between PMOs, and then, allow communities of PMOs emerging. This requires that the managers create environments, which allow developing a sense of community.
3. The triangle of roles can also be used as a tool for self-assessment of the relationships between PMOs in their particular situations.

Implications for academics:

1. This research situated the problem of PMO networks and their governance as a project management organizational design problem, following previous trends in PMO research (e.g., Hobbs & Aubry, 2010; Pellegrinelli & Garagna, 2009). In the future, other approaches to the problem may lead to some different insights in understanding this phenomenon. For example, the power system, stakeholders, different network structures, etc.
2. Theoretical background: basically, this research relies on three complementary theoretical foundations that altogether provide a rich understanding of a rather complex phenomenon: network theory, community of practices theory and governance. This pluralism in the theoretical approach was required to make sense of this complex phenomenon. It follows Denis et al. (2007) and more recently Greenwood and Miller (2010) in combining multiple theoretical perspective to understand complex phenomena. Future research could explore this combination in more depth.
3. A mixed method approach was used in this research. Yet it contributes to the current thread of this type of research (e.g., Aubry et al., 2011), which combined two or more methodological approaches to provide multiple facets of a complex phenomenon, such as communities of PMOs. As shown here, case studies provide rich context descriptions and in-depth understanding of each individual situation. These were subsequently compared and analyzed. SNA confirmed and explained limitations in the relationships between PMOs which otherwise would have been hidden.

This first research on multiple PMOs in large organization delivered interesting results that the authors hope will be taken further in the near future.

APPENDICES

Appendix A

PMO Research—Invitation to Engage

Governance and Communities of PMOs

Aims and Objectives

Project Management Institute (PMI) has commissioned a research team from the University of Quebec, Canada and Umeå University, Sweden to undertake a research project to assess networks of Project Management Offices (PMOs). That includes, but is not limited to, the organization of PMOs, sharing of roles and responsibilities within PMO networks, their interaction and governance. The aim is to develop an integrated model of PMO networks within large organizations. This model will support practitioners and upper management in pursuing existing and articulating new strategies and structure for delivery of maximum project management value.

Background

PMOs are frequently found in large organizations. Increasingly, PMOs are created at various levels in the organizational hierarchy or network. However, there is extreme variety in the PMO structure, mandate and functions they fulfill. In addition to that PMOs frequently transform in terms of their structure and mandate. Other organizational units often coexist with PMOs, with some of them sharing project management governance tasks with the PMO. Altogether, these entities are used to implement corporate objectives through projects in order to maximize value.

Past research looked at the different entities in isolation. The present research looks at the interaction and joint accomplishments of these units, mainly in terms of the joint work of different PMOs (or entities with similar mandates) as a network within the wider organization.

Areas of Investigation

The following questions are addressed through this research:

- How can communities of PMOs be described?
- Why do communities of PMOs get formed?
- Do PMOs relate to each other and if so, why?

- What are the related project governance mechanisms?
- What links PMOs and project management governance?

Engagement Process:

If you choose to participate in this research, the engagement process is as follows:

- One introductory meeting with a representative of the research team in order to understand your current organizational structure as it relates to PMOs. Typically no more than 1 hour in duration, that will allow for identification and agreement on the types and number of PMOs to be interviewed.
- Interview with three (desirable) or two (minimum) representatives of each PMO. These should be the Supervisor of the Head of the PMO (desirable), the Head of the PMO and a PMO member (minimum). Each interview will last about 60 minutes. This will allow the questions to be explored in more detail and uncover some initial findings.
- Collection of data from the interviewed PMO, its related projects and team members using an Excel spreadsheet. That will allow for a Social Network Analysis, which constructs topological networks for analysis of positions and roles of PMOs as well as the overall structure of linkages within the community of PMO network.

The results of the study will later be validated through a worldwide web-based survey. Feedback on the results from the research will be provided through a briefing session and summary report.

Confidentiality:

The nature of the engagement is such that no information with respect to any business conducted by any participants will be disclosed, directly or indirectly.

Appendix B

Communities of PMOs Interview Guide — General[3]

1. **Tell me about the your company**
2. **Tell me about your role in relation to project management and PMOs**
   a. How strong is project management in your company?

3. **Projects**
   a. What are the types of projects you do?
   b. How do you assess the performance of projects within your mandate?

4. **The Project Management Office**
   a. What is the mission (objectives) of the PMO?
   b. What does your PMO do? [concrete tasks]
   c. Is it the first implementation? Why has it been implemented or changed?
   d. How is this PMO different from other ones in the organization?
   e. What are your relations with other PMOs? What are you doing together?
   f. Which parts of your projects are realized without collaboration with other PMOs

5. **Community of PMOs**
   a. Does a community of PMOs exists in your organization?
   b. If yes, why, how and by whom was it established?
   c. If not—why?

6. **Employee**
   a. Tell me about employees of your PMO (competence area, work climate, controller versus adviser, etc.)
   b. How would you qualify the relationship between employees from different PMOs?

---

[3] This guide may have to be adapted for specific role around PMO.

7. **Governance**
    a. How do you collaborate with other PMOs?
    b. Is there a central management or coordination of PMOs?
    c. How do you synchronize between PMOs
        i. Charters
        ii. Objectives
        iii. Incentives
        iv. Responsibilities
        v. People/skills
        vi. Authority
        vii. Governance of projects
        viii. emergencies
    d. Is your organization more process (compliance) or more outcome (results) oriented?
    e. Related to the question above. Is the work of yours and other PMOs in alignment with the organizational governance approach?
    f. Is your organization more stakeholder oriented or more shareholder oriented?
    g. Do you have policies, processes, etc., for PMO work, organizations, roles, and responsibilities?

8. **Closure**
    Do you have any comments to add that would help our understanding on PMOs in your organization?

Appendix C

Network Survey Questionnaire

1. **What is your name?**
   (Please choose your name from the list)

2. **Please list as many people as you consider important inside the company for providing you with expertise related to project management. Please check twice that you have not forgotten anyone from whom you received relevant PM knowledge.**
   Please insert the name of these persons. Your input will be automatically completed.

3. **What is your current position at this company?**
   (Please choose the position from the list.)

4. **In what year did you take this position?**
   (Please choose the year from the list.)

5. **At what position did you start at this company?**
   (Please choose the position from the list.)

6. **In what business function do you work?**
   R&D
   Production
   Sales
   Marketing
   Administrative functions

7. **Which premise do you work in? What plant level do you work on?**
   The building for R&D and Quality Check
   The building for Preparation and Production
   The building for Communication

8. **What is the total number of projects that you have worked on during your employment with this company?**
   Number of a-projects:
   Number of b-projects:
   Number of c-projects:

9. **How many of these projects have you directed as PM?**
   Number of a-projects:
   Number of b-projects:
   Number of c-projects:

10. **In what year did you first take the role as a project manager?**
    (Please choose the year from the list.)

11. **Are you a member of the PMO team?**

12. **Have you ever been a member of the expert group in the Project Management Office?**
    If so, for how many months in total?

13. **What is the particular expertise that your colleagues usually ask for when they seek your advice?**

14. **Do you agree with the following statements? (6 point scale of agreement)**
    - I do not need any help from the PMO at this company.
    - My fellow PMs have adopted and used parts of my project management know-how to improve their project management practice.
    - I am eager to help my fellow PMs whenever they need advice.
    - I do not need any help from my fellow PMs.
    - My fellow PMs turn to me frequently to seek my advice.
    - The PMO support has proved effective for my projects over the last years.
    - I would like to see more knowledge exchange and contact with other project managers at this company.
    - Exchanging more knowledge between project managers at this company would increase the performance of the company.
    - I have benefited from the PMO at this company.
    - My projects would have produced the same results without the PMO at this company

15. **Which support did you receive from the PMO at this company?**
    Please provide some key words

16. **Have you had the chance to suggest new best practices (e.g., tools, techniques, concepts) to the PMO? Which best practices? Please indicate or describe these in key words.**

17. **Where do you currently see critical barriers to a more effective knowledge exchange in the company?**

18. **Do you have any suggestions on how to improve the exchange of project management knowledge within this company?**

19. **Within this company, who are the persons who have provided signifi-cant expertise to help you solve project management-related problems over the last years?**
Please check twice that you have not forgotten anyone from whom you received relevant PM knowledge. (Please insert the name of these persons. Your input will be automatically completed).

20. **Apart from your native language, in what other languages do you have full proficiency in writing and speaking?**
English
French
Spanish
other (please specify)

21. **In what year did you join the company?**
Please choose the year from the list.

22. **Who is your direct supervisor that you report to?**
Please choose your name from the list.
If not included in the list above, please indicate the full name of your supervisor (family name, given name):

23. **What is your educational background?**
business/economics
engineering
information systems
chemistry/pharamaceuticals
social science
natural sciences
other

24. **Please indicate your highest degree of education.**
primary school
secondary school
college/university degree (Bachelor)
postgraduate degree (Master)
PhD/Doctor

References

Abril, R., & Müller, R. (2009). Lessons learned as organizational project memories. In J. Girard (Ed.), *Building organizational memories: Will we know what we knew?* (pp. 97–114). New York, NY: Information Science Reference.

Almeida, P., & Kogut, B. (1999). Localization of knowledge and the mobility of engineers in regional networks. *Management Science, 45*(7), 905–917.

Archer, M., Bhaskar, R., Collier, A., Lawson, T., & Norrie, A. (1998). *Critical realism.* London, UK: Routledge.

Arthur, M. B., DeFillippi, R. J., & Jones, C. (2001). Project-based learning as the interplay of career and company non-financial capital. *Management Learning, 32*(1), 99–117.

Artto, K., Kulvik, I., Poskela, J., & Turkulainen, V. (2011). The integrative role of the project management office in the front end of innovation. *International Journal of Project Management, 29*(4), 408–421.

Association for Project Management. (2004). *Directing change: A guide to governance of project management.* High Wycombe, UK: Association for Project Management.

ATLAS.ti Software Development. (2004). ATLAS.ti. Berlin, Germany: Scientific Software Development. Retrieved from www.atlas.ti.com

Aubry, M. (2009, October 11–13). *Organisational project management: An approach based on actor network theory.* Paper presented at the International Research Network on Organizing by Projects (IRNOP IX) Conference, Berlin, Germany.

Aubry, M., & Hobbs, B. (2011). A fresh look at the contribution of project management to organizational performance. *Project Management Journal, 42*(1), 3–16.

Aubry, M., Hobbs, B., Müller, R., & Blomquist, T. (2011). *Identifying the forces driving the frequent changes in PMOs.* Newtown Square, PA: Project Management Institute.

Aubry, M., Hobbs, B., & Thuillier, D. (2007). A new framework for understanding organisational project management through PMO. *International Journal of Project Management, 25*(4), 328–336.

Aubry, M., Müller, R., & Glückler, J. (2010, July 11–14). *Exploring PMOs through community of practice theory.* Paper presented at the PMI Research Conference, Washington, DC.

Aubry, M., Müller, R., Hobbs, B., & Blomquist, T. (2011). Project management offices in transition. *International Journal of Project Management, 28*(8), 766–778.

Aubry, M., Richer, M.-C., Lavoie-Tremblay, M., & Cyr, G. (in press). Pluralism in PMO performance: The case of a PMO dedicated to a major organizational transformation. *Project Management Journal.*

Bechara, J., & Van de Ven, A. H. (2011). Triangulating philosophies of science to understand complex organizational and managerial problems. In H. Tsoukas & R. Chia (Eds.), *Philosophy and organization theory* (pp. 312–342). Bingly, UK: Emerald Books.

Bellini, E., & Canonico, P. (2008). Knowing communities in project driven organizations: Analysing the strategic impact of socially constructed HRM practices. *International Journal of Project Management, 26*(1), 44–50.

Bhaskar, R. (1975). *A realistic theory of science.* Leeds, UK: Leeds Book Ltd.

Biedenbach, T., & Müller, R. (2011). Paradigms in project management research: Examples from 15 years of IRNOP conferences. *International Journal of Managing Projects in Business, 4*(1), 82–104.

Biedenbach, T., & Söderholm, A. (2008). The challenge of organizing change in hyper-competitive industries: A literature review. *Journal of Change Management, 8*(2), 123–145.

Blomquist, T., & Müller, R. (2006). Practices, roles, and responsabilities of middle managers in program and portfolio management. *Project Management Journal, 37*(1), 52–66.

Borgatti, S., & Carley, K. M. (2006). On the robustness of centrality measures under conditions of imperfect data. *Social Networks, 28*(2), 124–136.

Bredillet, C. N. (2004). Projects: Learning at the edge of organization. In P. W. G. Morris & J. K. Pinto (Eds.), *The Wiley guide to managing projects* (pp. 1112–1136). Hoboken, NJ: Wiley.

Bredillet, C., Yatim, F., & Ruiz, P. (2010). Project management deployment: The role of cultural factors. *International Journal of Project Management, 28*(2), 183–193.

Breschi, S., & Lissoni, F. (2009). Mobility of skilled workers and co-invention networks: An anatomy of localized knowledge flows. *Journal of Economic Geography, 9*(4), 439–468.

Bresnen, M., Edelman, L., Newell, S., Scarbrough, H., & Swan, J. (2003). Social practices and the management of knowledge in project environments. *International Journal of Project Management, 21*(3), 157–166.

Brookes, N. J., Morton, S. C., Dainty, A. R. J., & Burns, N. D. (2006). Social processes, patterns and practices and project knowledge management: A theoretical framework and an empirical investigation. *International Journal of Project Management, 24*(6), 474–482.

Brown, J. S., & Duguid, P. (1998). Organizing knowledge. *California Management Review, 40*(3), 90–111.

Brown, J. S., & Duguid, P. (2001). Knowledge and organization: A social-practice perspective. *Organization Science, 12*(2), 198–213.

Brown, S. L., & Eisenhardt, K. M. (1997). The art of continuous change: Linking complexity theory and time-paced evolution in relentlessly shifting organizations. *Administrative Science Quarterly, 42*(1), 1–34.

Burns, T., & Stalker, G. M. (1994). *The management of innovation.* Oxford, UK: Oxford University Press.

Burt, R. (1992). *Structural holes: The social structure of competition.* Cambridge, MA: Harvard University Press.

Clarke, T. (2004). The stakeholder corporation: A business philosophy for the information age. In T. Clarke (Ed.), *Theories of corporate governance: The philosophical foundations of corporate governance* (pp. 189–202). London, UK: Routledge.

Clegg, S. R., Pitsis, T. S., Rura-Polley, T., & Marosszeky, M. (2002). Governmentality matters: Designing an alliance culture of inter-organizational collaboration for managing projects. *Organization Studies (Walter de Gruyter GmbH & Co. KG.), 23*(3), 317–337.

Community. (n.d.). In *Merriam-Webster's Collegiate Dictionary* (11th ed.). Springfield, MA: Merriam-Webster.

Costenbader, E., & Valente, T. (2003). The stability of centrality measures when networks are sampled. *Social Networks, 25*(4), 283–307.

Crawford, J. K. (2010). *The strategic project office* (2nd ed.). Boca Raton, FL: CRC Press.

Crawford, L. (2010, May 19–22). *Deconstructing the PMO.* Paper presented at the EURAM Conference, Rome, Italy.

Dai, C. X. Y., & Wells, W. G. (2004). An exploration of project management office features and their relationship to project performance. *International Journal of Project Management, 22*(7), 523–532.

Day, G. S., & Schoemaker, P. J. H. (2000). Avoiding the pitfalls of emerging technologies. In G. S. Day & P. J. H. Schoemaker (Eds.), *Wharton on Managing Emerging Technologies* (pp. 24–55). Danvers, MA: John Wiley and Sons Inc.

Denis, J.-L., Langley, A., & Rouleau, L. (2007). Strategizing in pluralistic contexts: Rethinking theoretical frames. *Human Relations, 60*(1), 179–215.

Dietrich, P., Artto, K., & Kujala, J. (2010, July 11–14). *Strategic priorities and PMO functions in project-based firms.* Paper presented at the PMI Research Conference, Washington, DC.

DiMaggio, P. J., & Powell, W. W. (1983). The iron cage revisited: Institutional isomorphism and collective rationality in organizational fields. *American Sociology Review, 48*(avril), 147–160.

Doloi, H. K. (2011). Understanding stakeholders' perspective of cost estimation in project management [Article]. *International Journal of Project Management, 29*(5), 622–636.

Duguid, P. (2008a).·Prologue: Community of practice then and now. In A. Amin & J. Roberts (Eds.), *Community, economic creativity, and organization* (pp. 1–10). Oxford, UK: Oxford University Press.

Duguid, P. (2008b). "The art of knowing:" Social and tacit dimensions of knowledge and the limits of the community of practice. In A. Amin & J. Roberts (Eds.), *Community, economic creativity, and organization* (pp. 69–89). Oxford, UK: Oxford University Press.

Eisenhardt, K. M. (1989). Building theories from case study research. *Academy of Management Review, 14*(4), 532–550.

Eisenhardt, K. M., & Graebner, M. E. (2007). Theory building from cases: Opportunities and challenges. *Academy of Management Journal, 50*(1), 25–32.

Engwall, M. (2003). No project is an island: Linking projects to history and context. *Research Policy, 32*(5), 789–808.

Fernie, S., Green, S. D., Weller, S. J., & Newcombe, R. (2003). Knowledge sharing: Context, confusion and controversy. *International Journal of Project Management, 21*(3), 177–187.

Freeman, E. R., Harrison, J. S., Wicks, A. C., Parmar, B. L., & De Colle, S. (2010). *Stakeholder theory: The state of the art.* Cambridge, UK: Cambridge University Press.

Galbraith, J. R. (1977). *Organization design*. Reading, MA: Addison-Wesley Publishing Company.

Gertler, M. S. (2003). Tacit knowledge and the economic geography of context, or the undefinable tacitness of being (there). *Journal of Economic Geography, 3*(1), 75–99.

Gibson, C. B., & Birkinshaw, J. (2004). The antecedents, consequences, and mediating role of organizational ambidexterity. *The Academy of Management Journal, 47*(2), 209–226.

Glaser, B., & Strauss, A. L. (1967). *The discovery of grounded theory: Strategies for qualitative research*. Chicago, IL: Aldine Pub.

Glückler, J. (2008). Die chancen der standortspaltung: Wissensnetze im globalen unternehmen. *Geographische Zeitschrift, 96*, 125–139.

Glückler, J. (2010). Netzwerkforschung in der Geographie. In C. Stegbauer & R. Häußling (Eds.), *Handbuch netzwerkforschung* (pp. 873–881). Wiesbaden, Germany: VS Verlag.

Glückler, J. (2011). Islands of expertise: Global knowledge transfer in a technology service firm. In H. Bathelt, M. Feldman, & D.-F. Kogler (Eds.), *Beyond territory: Dynamic geographies of innovation and knowledge creation* (pp. 207–26). London, UK: Routledge.

Graham, D. J., & Midgley, N. G. (2000). Graphical representation of particle shape using triangular diagrams: An Excel spreadsheet method. *Earth Surface Processes and Landforms, 25*(13), 1473–1477.

Granovetter, M. (2005). The impact of social structure on economic outcomes. *Journal of Economic Perspectives, 19*(1), 33–50

Greenwood, R., & Miller, D. (2010). Tackling design anew: Getting back to the heart of organizational theory. *Academy of Management Perspectives, 24*(4), 78–88.

Hagström, P., Sölvell, Ö., & Hedlund, G. (1999). A three-dimensional model of changing internal structure in the firm. In A. D. Chandler, Jr., P. Hagström & O. Solvell (Eds.), *The dynamic firm: The role of technology, strategy, organization, and regions* (pp. 166–191). New York, NY: Oxford University Press.

Hansen, M. T. (2002). Knowledge networks: Explaining effective knowledge sharing in multiunit companies. *Organization Science, 13*(3), 232–248.

Hedlund, G. (1994). A model of knowledge management and the N-Form corporation. *Strategic Management Journal, 15*(Summer), 73–90.

Hobbs, B., & Aubry, M. (2008). An empirically grounded search for a typology of project management offices. *Project Management Journal, 39*(S1), S69–S82.

Hobbs, B., & Aubry, M. (2010). *The project management office: A quest for understanding*. Newtown Square, PA: Project Management Institute.

Hobbs, B., & Aubry, M. (2011, June 19–22). *A typology of PMOs derived using cluster analysis and the relationship with performance*. Paper presented at the International Research Network on Organizing by Projects (IRNOP) Conference, Montreal, Canada.

Hobbs, B., Aubry, M., & Thuillier, D. (2008). The project management office as an organisational innovation. *International Journal of Project Management, 26*(5), 547–555.

Huemann, M. (2010). Considering human resource management when developing a project-oriented company: Case study of a telecommunication company. *International Journal of Project Management, 28*(4), 361–369.

Hughes, P. T. (1987). The evolution of large technological systems. In W. E. Bijker, T. P. Hughes, & T. J. Pinch (Eds.), *The social construction of technological systems: New directions in the sociology and history of technology* (pp. 51–81). Cambridge, MA: MIT Press.

Hurt, M., & Thomas, J. L. (2009). Building value through sustainable project management offices. *Project Management Journal, 40*(1), 55–72.

Information Systems Audit and Control Association (ISACA). (1998). *COBIT: Governance, control and audit for information and related technology.* Rolling Meadows, IL: ISACF.

Island. (n.d.). In *Merriam-Webster's Collegiate Dictionary* (11th ed.). Springfield, MA: Merriam-Webster.

Jensen, M. C. (2000). *A theory of the firm: Governance, residual claims, and organizational forms.* Cambridge, MA: Harvard University Press.

Jensen, M. C., & Meckling, W. H. (1976). Theory of the firm: Managerial behavior, agency costs, and ownership structure. *Journal of Financial Economics, 3*(4), 305–360.

Jones, C., Hesterly, W. S., & Borgatti, S. P. (1997). A general theory of network governance: Exchange conditions and social mechanisms. *Academy of Management Review, 22*(4), 911–945.

Keegan, A., & Turner, R. J. (2001). Quantity versus quality in project-based learning practices. *Management Learning, 32*(1), 77–98.

Kilduff, M., Mehra, A., & Dunn, M. B. (2011). From blue sky research to problem solving: A philosophy of science theory of new knowledge production. *Academy of Management Review, 36*(2), 297–317.

Kilduff, M., & Tsai, W. (2003). *Social networks and organizations.* London, UK: Sage.

Klakegg, O. J., Williams, T., Magnussen, O. M., & Glasspool, H. (2008). Governance frameworks for public project development and estimation. *Project Management Journal, 39*, S27–S42.

Kotnour, T. (1999). A learning framework for project management. *Project Management Journal, 30*(2), 32–38.

Kotnour, T. (2000). Organizational learning practices in the project management environment. *The International Journal of Quality & Reliability Management, 17*(4/5), 393–406.

Krackhardt, D. (1990). Assessing the political landscape: Structure, cognition, and power in organizations. *Administrative Science Quarterly, 35*, 342–369.

Langley, A. (1999). Strategies for theorizing from process data. *Academy of Management Review, 24*(4), 691–710.

Larson, E. (2004). Project management structures. In P. W. G. Morris & J. K. Pinto (Eds.), *The Wiley guide to managing projects* (pp. 48–66). Hoboken, NJ: John Wiley & Sons, Inc.

Lave, J. (2008). Epilogue: Situated learning and changing practice. In A. Amin & J. Roberts (Eds.), *Community, economic creativity, and organization* (pp. 283–296). Oxford, UK: Oxford University Press.

Lave, J., & Wenger, E. (1991). *Situated learning: Legitimate peripheral participation.* New York, NY: Cambridge University Press.

Lazega, E. (2000). Rule enforcement among peers: A lateral control regime. *Organisation Studies, 21*(1), 193–214.

Lazega, E. (2001). *The collegial phenomenon: The social mechanisms of cooperation among peers in a corporate law partnership.* Oxford, UK: Oxford University Press.

Lundin, R. A., & Söderholm, A. (1995). A theory of the temporary organization. *Scandinavian Journal of Management, 11*(4), 437–455.

March, J. G. (1991). Exploration and exploitation in organizational learning. *Organization Science, 2*(1), 71–87.

Marsden, P. V. (1990). Network data and measurement. *Annual Review of Sociology, 16*, 435–463.

Marsden, P. V. (2003). Interviewer effects in measuring network size using a single name generator. *Social Networks, 25*(1), 1–16.

Maylor, H., Brady, T., Cooke-Davies, T., & Hodgson, D. (2006). From projectification to programmification. *International Journal of Project Management, 24*(8), 663–674.

McPhee, R. D., & Poole, M. S. (2000). Organizational structures and configurations. In F. M. Jablin & L. L. Putnam (Eds.), *The new handbook of organizational communication* (pp. 503–543). London, UK: Sage Publications.

Mead, S. P. (2001). Using social network analysis to visualize project teams. *Project Management Journal, 32*(4), 32–38.

Miles, M. B., & Huberman, A. M. (1994). *Qualitative data analysis: A source book of new methods.* Beverly Hills, CA: Sage Publications.

Miles, R. E., Snow, C. C., Mathews, J. A., Miles, G., & Coleman, H. J., Jr. (1997). Organizing in the knowledge age: Anticipating the cellular form. *The Academy of Management Executive, 11*(4), 7–21.

Miller, R., & Hobbs, B. (2005). Governance regimes for large complex projects. *Project Management Journal, 36*(3), 42–50.

Mintzberg, H. (1989). *Mintzberg on management: Inside our strange world of organizations.* New York: The Free Press.

Mitchell, J. C. (1969). The Concept and use of social network. In J. C. Mitchell (Ed.), *Social networks in urban situations: Analysis of personal relationships in central african towns* (pp. 1–50). Manchester, UK: Manchester University Press.

Morabito, J., Sack, I., & Bhate, A. (1999). *Modeling organization: Innovative architectures for the 21st century.* Upper Saddle River, NJ: Prentice Hall.

Müller, R. (2009). *Governance in projects.* Aldershot, UK: Gower Publishing.

Müller, R. (2011). Project governance. In P. W. G. Morris, J. K. Pinto, & J. Söderlund (Eds.), *The Oxford handbook of project management* (pp. 297–320). Oxford, UK: Oxford University Press.

Müller, R., Aubry, M., & Glückler, J. (2011, June 19–22). *A relational typology of project management offices.* Paper presented at the IRNOP, Montreal, Canada.

Nohria, N. (1992). Is a network perspective a useful way of studying organizations? In N. Nohria & R. G. Eccles (Eds.), *Networks and organizations: Structure, form and action* (pp. 1–22). Boston, MA: Harvard Business School Press.

Nonaka, I., & Takeuchi, H. (1995). *The knowledge-creating company*. New York, NY: Oxford University Press.

Nonaka, I., & von Krogh, G. (2009). Tacit knowledge and knowledge conversion: Controversy and advancement in organizational knowledge creation theory. [Article]. *Organization Science, 20*(3), 635–652.

Office of Government Commerce. (2005). *Managing successful projects with PRINCE2*. London, UK: The Stationary Office [TSO].

Office of Government Commerce. (2009). Successful delivery pocketbook. Retrieved from http://www.ogc.gov.uk

Organisation for Economic Co-operation and Development. (2004). *OECD Principles of Corporate Governance*. Paris: OECD Publishing.

Ouchi, W. G. (1977). The relationship between organizational structure and organizational control [Article]. *Administrative Science Quarterly, 22*(1), 95–113.

Ouchi, W. G. (1978). The transmission of control through organizational hierarchy. *Academy of Management Journal, 21*(2), 173–192.

Ouchi, W. G., & Maguire, M. A. (1975). Organizational control: Two functions [Article]. *Administrative Science Quarterly, 20*(4), 559–569.

Patterson, L., Urban, M., Myers, A., Bhaduri, B., Bright, E., & Coleman, P. (2007). Assessing spatial and attribute errors in large national datasets for population distribution models: A case study of Philadelphia County schools. *GeoJournal, 69*(1), 93–102.

Patton, M. Q. (2002). *Qualitative research & evaluation methods*. Thousand Oaks, CA: Sage Publications.

Pellegrinelli, S., & Garagna, L. (2009). Towards a conceptualisation of pmos as agents and subjects of change and renewal. *International Journal of Project Management, 27*(7), 649–656.

Pellegrinelli, S., Partington, D., Hemingway, C., Mohdzain, Z., & Shah, M. (2007). The importance of context in programme management: An empirical review of programme practices. *International Journal of Project Management, 25*(1), 41–55.

Pettigrew, A. M., & Massini, S. (2003). Innovative forms of organizing: Trends in Europe, Japan and the USA in the 1990s. In A. M. Pettigrew, R. Whittington, L. Melin, C. Sanchez-Runde, F. A. J. Van den Bosch, W. Ruigrok, & T. Numagami (Eds.), *Innovative forms of organizing* (pp. 1–33). London, UK: Sage Publications.

Pinto, A., Cota, M., & Levin, G. (2010, July 11-14). *The PMO maturity cube, a project management management office maturity model*. Paper presented at the PMI Research Conference, Washington, DC.

Plewe, B., & Bagchi-Sen, S. (2001). The use of weighted ternary histograms for the visualization of segregation. *Professional Geographer, 53*(3), 347–360.

Podolny, J. M., & Page, K. L. (1998). Network forms of organization. *Annual Review of Sociology, 24*, 57–76.

Powell, W. W. (1990). Neither market nor hierarchy: Networks forms of organizations. *Research in Organizational Behavior, 12*, 295–336.

Powell, W. W., Koput, K. W., & Smith-Doerr, L. (1996). Interorganizational collaboration and the locus of innovation: Networks of learning in biotechnology. *Administrative Science Quarterly, 41*(1), 116–145.

Practice. (n.d.). In *Merriam-Webster's Collegiate Dictionary* (11th ed.). Springfield, MA: Merriam-Webster.

Preusser, H. (1976). Entwicklung und räumliche differenzierung der bevölkerung Islands. *Geografiska Annaler. Series B, Human Geography, 58*(2), 116–144.

Project Management Association of Japan. (2008). *Project & program management (P2M): Project and program management for enterprise innovation.* Tokyo, Japan: Project Management Association of Japan.

Project Management Institute. (2008). *A guide to the project management body of knowledge (PMBOK® Guide)* (4th ed.). Newtown Square, PA: Project Management Institute.

Provan, K. G., & Kenis, P. (2008). Modes of network governance: Structure, management, and effectiveness. *Journal of Public Administration Research & Theory, 18*(2), 229–252.

Pryke, S. D. (2005). Towards a social network theory of project governance. *Construction Management & Economics, 23*(9), 927–939.

Pryke, S., & Pearson, S. (2006). Project governance: Case studies on financial incentives. *Research and Information, 34*(6), 534–545.

Rank, O. N., Robins, G. L., & Pattison, P. E. (2010). Structural logic of intraorganizational networks. *Organization Science, 21*(3), 745–764.

Reagans, R., & McEvily, B. (2003). Network structure and knowledge transfer: The effects of cohesion and range. *Administrative Science Quarterly, 48*(2), 240–267.

Saunders, M., Lewis, P., & Thornhill, A. (2007). *Research methods for business students.* Harlow, UK: Pearson Education Limited.

Sayer, A. (2000). *Realism and social science.* London, UK: Sage Publications.

Sayer, A. (2001). For a critical cultural political economy. *Antipode, 33*(4), 687–708.

Scarbrough, H., & Swan, J. (2008). Project work as a locus of learning: The journey through practice. In A. Amin & J. Roberts (Eds.), *Community, economic creativity, and organization* (pp. 148–177). Oxford, UK: Oxford University Press.

Schnell, R., Hill, P., & Esser, E. (1995). *Methoden der empirischen sozialforschung.* München, Wien: Oldenbourg.

Schön, D. A. (1983). *The reflexive practitioner: How professionals thinks in action.* New York, NY: Basic Books.

Scott, J. (2000). *Social network analysis: A handbook* (2nd ed.). London, UK: Sage Publications.

Sense, A. J., & Badham, R. J. (2008). Cultivating situated learning within project management practice. *International Journal of Managing Projects in Business, 1*(3), 432–438.

Shenhar, A., Dvir, D., Milosevic, D., Mulenburg, J., Patanakul, P., Reilly, R., & Thamhain, H. (2005). Toward a NASA-specific project management framework. *Engineering Management Journal, 17*(4), 8–16.

Söderlund, J. (2010). Pluralism in project management: Navigating the crossroads of specialization and fragmentation. *International Journal of Management Reviews, 13*(2), 153–176.

Software Engineering Institute. (2011). Capability maturity model integration. Retrieved from http://www.sei.cmu.edu/cmmi/

Sorenson, O., & Waguespack, D. M. (2006). Social Structure and exchange: Self-confirming dynamics in Hollywood. *Administrative Science Quarterly, 51(4)*, 560–589.

Tashakkori, A., & Teddlie, C. (1998). *Mixed methodologies.* Thousand Oaks, CA: Sage Publications.

Tashakkori, A., & Teddlie, C. (2010). Issues and dilemnas in teaching research methods courses in social and behavioural sciences: U.S. perspectives. *International Journal of Social Reseach Methodology, 6*(1), 61–77.

Teddlie, C., & Yu, F. (2007). Mixed methods sampling: A typology with examples. *Journal of Mixed Methods Research, 1*(1), 77–100.

Ter Wal, A. L. J., & Boschma, R. A. (2009). Applying social network analysis in economic geography: Framing some key analytic issues. *The Annals of Regional Science, 43*, 739–756.

Tsai, W. (2001). Knowledge transfer in intraogranizational networks: Effects of network position and absorptive capacity on business unit innovation and performance. *Academy of Management Journal, 44*(5), 996–1004.

Tsaturyan, T. (2010). *Integration in project governance (Master's thesis).* Stockholm University, Sweden.

Turner, R. J., & Keegan, A. E. (1999). The versatile project-based organization: Governance and operational control. *European Management Journal, 17*(3), 296–309.

Turner, R. J., & Keegan, A. E. (2001). Mechanisms of governance in the project-based organization: Roles of the broker and steward. *European Management Journal, 19*(3), 254–267.

Turner, R. J., & Müller, R. (2003). On the nature of the project as a temporary organization. *International Journal of Project Management, 21*(1), 1–8.

Turner, J. R., & Müller, R. (2004). Communication and co-operation on projects between the project owner as principal and the project manager as agent. *European Management Journal, 22*(3), 327–336.

Unger, B., Gemünden, H. G., & Aubry, M. (2011, June 19–22). *The three roles of a project portfolio management office: The impact on portfolio management execution and success.* Paper presented at the International Research Network on Organizing by Projects (IRNOP) Conference 2011, Montreal, Canada.

Van de Ven, A. H. (2007). *Engaged scholarship: Creating knowledge for science and practice.* Oxford, UK: Oxford University Press.

Van de Ven, A. H., & Johnson, P. E. (2006). Knowledge for theory and practice. *Academy of Management Review, 31*(4), 802–821.

Wasserman, S., & Faust, K. (1994). *Social network analysis: Methods and applications.* Cambridge, UK: Cambridge University Press.

Wenger, E. (2000). Communities of practice and social learning systems. *Organization, 7*(2), 225–246.

Wenger, E., & Snyder, W. M. (2000). Community of practice: The organizational frontier. *Harvard Business Review, 78*(1), 139–145.

White, H. C. (2002). *Markets from networks: Socioeconomic models of production* (2nd ed.). Princeton, NJ: Princeton University Press.

White, H. C. (2008). *Identity & control: How social formations emerge* (2nd ed.). Princeton, NJ: Princeton University Press.

Williams, T. (2005). Assessing and moving on from the dominant project management discourse in the light of project overruns. *IEEE Transactions on Engineering Management, 52*(4), 497–508.

Williams, T. (2007). *Post-project reviews to gain effective lessons learned.* Newtown Square, PA: Project Management Institute.

Williams, T. (2008). How do organizations learn lessons from projects—and do they? *IEEE Transactions on Engineering Management, 55*(2), 248–266.

Williamson, O. E. (1975). *Markets and hierarchies: Analysis and antitrust implications.* New York, NY: Collier Macmillan.

Williamson, O. E. (1985). *The economic institutions of capitalism.* New York, NY: The Free Press.

Williamson, O. E. (1991). Comparative economic organization: The analysis of discrete structural alternatives. *Administrative Science Quarterly, 36*(2), 269–296.

Winch, G. M., Meunier, M.-C., & Head, J. (2010, May 19–22). *Projects as the content and process of change: The case of the health and safety laboratory.* Paper presented at the EURAM 2010, Rome, Italy.

Yin, R. K. (2009). *Case study research: Design and methods* (4th ed.). Thousand Oaks, CA: Sage Publications.